P9-DDE-084

CAT LOVERS

CAT LOVERS
A Compendium

Helena Chamberlain

METRO BOOKS
New York

METRO BOOKS
New York

An Imprint of Sterling Publishing Co., Inc.
1166 Avenue of the Americas
New York, NY 10036

METRO BOOKS and the distinctive Metro Books logo are registered trademarks of Sterling Publishing Co., Inc.

© 2019 Regency House Publishing Limited

All rights reserved. No part of this publication may be reproduced, stored in a retrieval system, or transmitted in any form or by any means (including electronic, mechanical, photocopying, recording, or otherwise) without prior written permission from the publisher.

ISBN 978-1-4351-6982-1

For information about custom editions, special sales, and premium and corporate purchases, please contact Sterling Special Sales at 800-805-5489 or specialsales@sterlingpublishing.com.

Manufactured in China

2 4 6 8 10 9 7 5 3 1

sterlingpublishing.com

CONTENTS

INTRODUCTION

The cat has had a close relationship with man since prehistoric times when they were first domesticated. For as long ago as 10,000 years, they have been greatly valued not only for vermin control but also for their beauty and companionship.

However, considering our long and successful relationship with the domestic feline, it is only relatively recently that man has manipulated the genetics of the species to create specific breeds. Most of us can identify some of the most famous breeds. You might recognize at least a few of the following: Persian, Maine Coon, Siamese, Abyssinian, Russian Blue, Tonkinese, and Burmese. These are, in fact, only a few of the 50 or so breeds recognized by the world's major cat registries. Moreover, there are a handful more that are quite new or rare and not yet officially recognized by many feline associations.

This beautifully photographed book describes the origins and characteristics of the cat, its evolution from wild animal to the perfect pet we know and love today. The book then goes on to provide valuable advice and guidance about all the aspects of cat ownership and care.

Chapter One
THE EVOLUTION
&
HISTORY OF THE CAT

Cats have been domesticated since prehistoric times, perhaps for as long as 10,000 years. Throughout human history, they have been greatly valued as destroyers of vermin, as well as for their ornamental qualities. However, considering our long and successful relationship with the domestic feline, the phenomenon of the pure-bred cat is a surprisingly recent one.

How many breeds of cats could you identify? The chances are that you might recognize at least a few of the following: Persian, Maine Coon, Siamese, Abyssinian, Russian Blue, Tonkinese, Burmese. These are, in fact, at least some of the 50 or so breeds recognized by the world's major cat registries. There are a handful more that are quite new or rare and not yet officially recognized by many feline associations.

Cats have graced us with their presence since the time of the ancient Egyptians, possibly much earlier. But it took the rise in popularity of cat shows in late 19th-century England to kick-start the selective breeding of the domestic cat into separate types. All but a few domestic cat breeds are less than 100 years old, and most of them appeared on the scene far more recently. Compare this to the dog world, where rudimentary selective breeding started several thousand years ago.

The Feline Group
The domestic cat is related to lions, tigers, pumas, and other wild cats, and the similarity in looks and behavior is immediately apparent. However, it is the smaller wildcat which is the cat's closest relative. The Scottish Wildcat is a fine example and its superb natural camouflage enables it to merge imperceptibly into the surrounding countryside. It is adaptable, hardy and extremely timid. Further south lives the Jungle Cat which, despite its name, inhabits the sandy desert regions of Egypt and has a beautifully ticked coat which blends in splendidly with the surrounding terrain. There are many other wildcats in evidence throughout the world, but due to extreme timidity, little is unfortunately known about them. In fact, wildcats appear in many places, in the snow-

LEFT: The Maine Coon is one of the largest and oldest breeds of cat in North America.

RIGHT: The domestic cat is closely related to all the other cat species in the world including the tiger.

ABOVE: The Scottish Wild Cat is one of several species of small cat. It is very closely related to the domestic cat.

enveloped north, in deserts and mountains, and in every case have managed to evolve to fit their environments. These adaptations have filtered through to our domestic breeds: for example, the Russian Blue is an inhabitant of the Baltic region of Europe, where the climate is predominately cold, so it fortunately came equipped with a dense, luxurious "double coat" to keep it warm. Likewise the Angora and Persians of upland Turkey and Iran also have thick coats valuable for keeping the cold at bay during the bitter continental nights. At the other extreme, the Oriental breeds have paler, silkier, and thinner coats, to reflect the heat of the tropics, and which keep them correspondingly cooler.

Feral cats live in organized groups, usually in the vicinity of human populations where they can either scavenge for food or rely on food provided for them by local people. The Colosseum in Rome has such a colony where people bring them food and their way of life has changed very little for centuries. Other groups such as Egyptian bazaar cats have an ancient lineage and are to this day highly respected by the local people.

Domestication

Remains of cats have been found from the pre-pottery Neolithic period of Jericho (circa 7000 BC), though these may have been hunted animals or the equivalent of modern feral cats, attracted to food scraps and at best tolerated. However, tamed cats have possibly lived in association with humans far earlier than archaeological and historical records imply. Cat remains (bones, teeth) are often retrieved from prehistoric sites, but it is impossible to know whether these were companions, or prey killed for their pelts and meat. Later, instead of hunting them, humans would have deliberately encouraged the presence of cats as rat catchers.

The ancient Egyptian domestic cat, which spread to Europe in historic times, was used as a retriever in hunting as well as for catching rats and mice. It was probably derived from *Felis lybica* or one of the other North African wildcats. The modern domestic cat is probably descended from this animal, perhaps with an admixture of other wildcat species, or of species domesticated at various times in other parts of the world. Once the Egyptians had given up the nomadic lifestyle and learned to till the soil, they settled into

CAT FACT

The oldest known pet cat was recently found in a 9,500-year-old grave on the Mediterranean island of Cyprus.

LEFT: Bastet was a cat goddess of the ancient Egyptians who created many statues of cats in her honor like this one.

agrarian communities. Since these communities depended for their very existence upon their crops, which could only be harvested once or twice a year, a means of storing them between harvests had to be found. Early on, this consisted merely of keeping grain in baskets. This attracted mice, rats, and other vermin, which attracted the local lesser cat, the African Wildcat. People started encouraging the cats to stay close by to catch the vermin by leaving out scraps. Since they had a ready source of food, no threat from the people, and an absence of enemies, cats moved in on a permanent basis. Being a naturally calm species, the African

ABOVE: It is believed that the cats of ancient Egypt were derived from North African wildcats such as this one.

ABOVE: In ancient Egyptian times, cats were often buried alongside their deceased owners.

Wildcat quickly adapted to people, allowing itself first to be approached, then petted, and eventually to be held. People began to appreciate the cat's other qualities: its nocturnal habits meant it hunted round the clock and, unlike the dog, it was a clean animal that buried its waste outside, away from its den.

In ancient Egypt, cats were not only established as domesticated animals, but were even cherished and worshipped as gods and religious idols. This was due to their status, in this agrarian society, as rat and mouse catchers. So cherished were they, that to kill a cat, even accidentally, was an offense punishable by death. If a house-cat died, the owners shaved off their eyebrows as a sign of mourning.

Numerous cat mummies have been found; many appear to have been sacrifices and cats would have been reared in large numbers for this purpose. Paintings would seem to suggest that cats were used in the hunting of wildfowl, although this is debatable since cats are not generally good retrievers. Later, they were depicted in paintings as symbols of fertility and/or domestic harmony.

Although ancient Egyptians forbade the export of cats, by 1700 BC the cat was being depicted in domestic scenes in the Holy Land. By 1400 BC domestic cats were present in Greece. By 1000 BC cats had traveled northwards across the Mediterranean aboard ships (possibly with Phoenician traders) and from there they spread along trade routes. The cat traveled eastward to China and Japan (where it protected silkworm cocoons from rats). In Japan, cats were so highly valued that they were not allowed out of the house, even when a plague of rodents threatened to devastate crops.

The Romans regarded cats as rare and exotic pets, preferring the mongoose for vermin control. By 500 BC, domestic cats seem to have been familiar in southern Europe. The cat may have arrived in England with the Phoenicians who traded for tin in Cornwall, though it is most likely that it was the Romans who first brought cats with them some time before AD 4. Further cats arrived with the Vikings.

During the early Middle Ages, the Norse goddess Freya was the closest thing to a cat goddess among the Europeans. She was constantly surrounded by cats and her worship contained many cat-oriented rituals. When Christians barred her worship, Freya became a demon and the cat became a manifestation of the devil. Cats became associated with witches and were even believed to be able to change form from cats to witches and back at will. Thus, being a symbol of Satan, cats were burned, killed and buried alive,

CAT FACT

During the Middle Ages, cats were associated with witchcraft, and were persecuted. They were put into sacks and tossed into bonfires.

Depending on the location and the century, black cats have been portrayed as either lucky or unlucky. Even today, there are may different beliefs associated with black cats across the world. In North America it is considered bad luck if a black cat crosses your path.

walled up in brick buildings, thrown off towers and tortured as part of religious rituals to drive out the devil.

The cat's popularity subsequently grew again, both on land and sea, because of its expertise in rodent control. Cats traveled alongside man in ships, valued as protectors of ships' supplies and as lucky mascots.

There was a very long period before the cat embarked on its voyage to the New World in any numbers. Although cats were taken to Quebec in the 1500s, and at least one cat accompanied the Pilgrim Fathers to America in 1620, it was not until the 1700s that domestic cats traveled to America with colonists and began to establish themselves on this continent. The cat penetrated Australia with Europeans in 1788, though aboriginal histories indicate that cats were already present on parts of the Australian coast as shipwreck survivors. There is no indigenous species of feline in Australia.

The History of Selective Breeding

During the 19th century, important advances began to be made in the knowledge of how diseases were able to spread. As a result, cats began to be favored as household pets in preference to dogs, being considered to be clean animals that are fastidious about their toilet. Domesticated cats interbred and in this way, almost by chance, people started to intervene in the selection and breeding of cats. Thus,

BELOW: The Siamese developed naturally in Thailand, formerly Siam, as early as the 14th century.

the first steps along the path of producing pedigree cats were taken.

The first major British cat show was held in London's Crystal Palace in 1871, and was organized by the writer and cat artist Harrison Weir. He wanted interested people to have the opportunity of observing the different colors, markings, and breeds of cat, and included newly imported Siamese cats, a Persian and an Abyssinian. The show was a huge success, and it became an annual event. Queen Victoria, who loved cats, acquired two Blue Persians. In 1887, the National Cat Club was formed, with Harrison Weir as its president, and registration procedures were instituted. This marked the beginning of the cat fancy as it is known today. The first cat show to attract wide attention in the USA took place at Madison Square Garden, New York, in 1895. In 1899, Weir published his book *Our Cats and All About Them*, in which he set out clear and concise standards of excellence, by which all the breeds and varieties could be judged.

The London and New York shows, and others in mainland Europe, proved an enormous success and were the main impetus for modern selective

ABOVE: During World War I and II, cat breeding suffered a setback and as a result many breeds such as the Russian Blue, pictured here, nearly became extinct.

breeding. The owners of pure-bred cats began to keep careful records, and so the first written pedigrees came into being. Groups interested in the same types of cats formed further clubs and societies. In 1896, the American Cat Club became North America's first registry to verify pedigrees.

At this time, the great majority of the world feline population was made up of the ubiquitous mixed-breed household cat. Breeders now began to search geographically isolated parts of the world for these products of natural selection for the purposes of cross-breeding. The cats they found included the Turkish Angora, Siamese, Russian Blue, Manx, and Abyssinian – all cats that had developed distinctive, recognizable traits setting them apart from others of their kind. These cats had developed, without human intervention, over the course of hundreds, and in some cases thousands of years.

During the 1900s, as travel became easier, breeds quickly spread across the world as it became increasingly popular to import cats from one country into another. Breeding suffered a setback during the two world wars, and some breeds, such as the Abyssinian and Russian Blue, nearly became extinct. From the late 1950s, the cat fancy expanded as knowledge of genetics grew, and many new breeds and color varieties within breeds were developed. Some of the new breeds, such as the Somali and the Balinese, are simply longhaired versions of older, shorthaired breeds. In some instances, genetic mutations were encouraged. In others, new breed characteristics arose through haphazard mutations, resulting in such traits as stub tails, abnormally short legs, bent or curled ears, curly hair or hairlessness. While a few mutations are crippling or deadly and others merely controversial, some are nevertheless deemed desirable, so these traits were deliberately isolated and developed over generations by cat breeders. However, human intervention is not responsible for some of the most distinctive mutations. The tailless Manx from the Isle of Man and the shortened tail of the Japanese Bobtail flourished because these cats had developed in geographic isolation.

There are some people who feel that encouraging mutations has gone too far, certainly as far as aesthetics are concerned, and there has been a recent trend away from highly exaggerated looks back towards more natural, wilder-looking cats that are more sympathetic to their ancestral roots.

RIGHT: The Somali is a longhaired breed closely related to the Abyssinian.

*"Of all God's creatures there is only one
that cannot be made a slave of the leash.
That one is the cat. If man could be crossed
with the cat it would improve man, but it
would deteriorate the cat."*

Mark Twain (1835–1910)

Chapter Two

THE WORLD
OF THE CAT

There are many different types of cat from which to choose, and they come in a variety of shapes and colors. The first choice is between pedigree and non-pedigree. Some people are attracted to pedigree cats because they admire certain characteristics which have become recognizable in a particular breed. For example, a Siamese may be preferred for its exotic appearance and flamboyant nature, or one might yearn for a Persian with its beautiful luxuriant coat. Unless you know of a particular kitten or cat at a rescue center, the best way of obtaining a pedigree cat is directly from a breeder. In this way you will be certain of the cat's origins, who has been caring for it, its medical history, and its parentage. Reputable breeders always ensure their cats are given a thorough health check by a vet, as well as the required inoculations for their ages before releasing them to new homes. Pedigree cats do not come cheap, so be prepared for a high price tag. Make

sure you read up on the breed of your choice as some are more prone to certain diseases than others. Take into account the amount of attention it may require; longhaired breeds need a thorough daily grooming session.

Pedigree cats tend to look more striking and exotic than their mixed-bred cousins, so bear in mind that the possibility of theft is correspondingly greater. For this reason, you may decide to construct a run in your garden to restrict your cat from roaming.

Should you decide that a non-pedigree is for you, you may have made a wise decision. They are robust, hardy, more resistant to disease than pedigree cats and are readily available from rescue centers. An attractive feature of non-pedigree cats is that although they are all beautiful, each one is unique and has its own particular characteristics.

RIGHT: Non-pedigree cats are just as beautiful and unique as their pedigree cousins. They are readily available from rescue centers, usually free of charge.

ABOVE: Pedigree breeds of cat come in many colors and combinations of colors. Originating in the United States in the 1960s, the Snowshoe has been selectively bred over time to enhance its striking coat and eye color.

Coat Color

The great variety in coat color is only possible in domestic cats because they do not rely on camouflage in order to survive. The attractive coloring of most pedigree cats would spell certain death if they were left to fend for themselves in the wild. Coat color is determined by pigment granules that occur in the shafts of each of the cat's hairs. Today, there are many variations in a cat's coat color, but they are all derived from only two pigments: black and red. Black was probably the first color mutation, followed by red and then white. A dilution of black to blue was brought about by a simple mutant gene, inherited as a recessive. The pigment granules within

the hair shafts are arranged in such a way that the animal appears to be slate-gray in color. This dilution gene also works on yellow pigmentation, changing it to cream, and on chocolate, changing it to lilac.

Cats with single-colored hair are called self or solid. Some coats are more dense and vibrant in some colors than in others. This occurs because the cat possesses a "dense" gene, which means that each hair strand is more densely packed with pigment, creating black, chocolate, cinnamon and red. Other cats have lighter, "dilute" coats in blue, lilac, fawn, and cream.

The dominant white gene contains no pigment to mask other colors, or combine with them to create a pattern. The white cat is genetically colored and it passes on this color potential to its offspring. The white gene is also associated with the deafness found in some blue-eyed, white-haired cats. The standard bi-

ABOVE: The Chinchilla is a specific type of Persian cat that has been selectively bred to have a white coat tipped with black. It has beautiful green eyes to match.

color is defined as being one-third to one-half white. "Bi-color" cats have white on their bellies and legs, but with patches of color on their heads and backs. The "Van" pattern is predominantly white but with solid patches on the head and tail only.

One of the most striking coats is the tortoiseshell, or "tortie" pattern, in which colored hairs occur in large distinct patches of red and black. Only female cats can have the tortoiseshell pattern because the gene can only be found on the X (female) chromosome. However, about one out of every 3,000 tri-color cats is a male and they are usually infertile.

Breed associations make things more complicated by giving the same genetic color a different name in different cats. For example, genetically chocolate Oriental Shorthairs are called Havana in the UK and Chestnut in North America. Meanwhile, tortie-and-

ABOVE: Bi-color cats such as this Ragdoll are usually one-third to one-half white, but have solid colors combined with the white.

white cats are called Calicos in some North American associations, while lilac cats in the UK are often called lavenders by US breeders. Differences in nomenclature are not restricted just to colors either, with Tabby Points being described as Lynx Points in North America.

Breeding standards for cats usually require the color of their lips, noses, and paw pads to correlate with coat color: pink in white cats, blue in blue cats, pink to brick red in reds. However, in some cases the specification can vary according to the particular breed or association.

ABOVE: This Siberian is a brown tabby. Despite being a pedigree, it has a similar coat color to the non-pedigree tabby. Siberians are known for their beautiful eye-color that can be green, gold, green-gold, or copper, although white Siberians can have blue or odd eyes (a different color in each eye).

Coat Pattern

When cats lived in the wild, their survival depended upon their ability to blend in with their environment. Used both for hiding and for hunting, this camouflage was typically a banded pattern, known as agouti, like that of a tabby cat, in the colors found in their natural environment.

"Underneath" every cat's coat – even those coats that appear to be solid colored – is the original tabby pattern designed to camouflage the cat in the wild, and a permanent reminder of the cat's roots. All other coat patterns are the result of genetic mutations that are encouraged through selective breeding. These mutations would have been dangerous to the cats when they lived in the wild, as their ability to hunt without being seen would have been seriously compromised. As pet cats, however, such considerations have been deemed irrelevant.

This tabby pattern known as agouti is named after a rodent of that name, which, along with other wild animals such as squirrels and mice, shares this patterning. In agouti patterning, each hair of the fur contains bands of color that are lighter at the base and darker towards the tip. These markings are what camouflage the cat in its environment. In domestic cats, they are often more apparent on kittens and gradually fade with maturity. Although the agouti gene is dominant, solid colors can exist in selectively bred cats because of the recessive non-agouti gene.

There are four basic patterns that result from the dominant tabby gene: Mackerel (also called striped), Classic (or blotched), Ticked (or Abyssinian), and Spotted. Mackerel stripes are narrow, parallel and run from the spine down the flanks to the belly. This pattern was predominant in Europe until a few hundred years ago, when it was superseded by the classic tabby pattern. Classic tabbies have wide stripes that form swirls on the flanks. The markings on ticked tabbies are restricted to the head, legs, and tail and the body is softly flecked.

Shading is the result of the "I," or inhibitor, gene. The I gene permits only the ends of the cat hair to retain pigment, resulting in subtle coat patterns that appear to change as the cat moves. In self cats, it

creates a "smoke" pattern, with a white undercoat. In agouti coats, the color is more restricted. Different degrees of shading create "shaded," "silver" and "silver tabby" coats, and "tipped" coats, which are only barely colored – known as "frosting." Another distinctive coat pattern is referred to as "pointing," most commonly seen in Siamese cats. The coat is light with dark areas, or "points," on the muzzle, ears, feet, and tail. In male cats, the hair is also darker on the scrotum. Interestingly, this coloring is temperature-sensitive: if skin temperature is lower, a special enzyme is activated that darkens the coat color. It is also affected by age, with Siamese kittens being pale at birth and then they often develop shading on their bodies in middle age, particularly in the case of darker varieties such as Seal Points.

BELOW: The Abyssinian has a ticked coat.

BELOW: This handsome Maine Coon is a silver tabby.

BELOW: Breeds such as the Norwegian Forest Cat originating in colder climates tend to be more stocky and solid with long, thick coats.

Body Form

A cat's facial features, body shape and other physical characteristics, such as folded ears, are more indicative of breed than the color or pattern of the coat, which are often similar across the different breeds. These physical characteristics developed as the breed adapted to its environment and can also be indicators of a breed's personality. For example, leaner breeds tend to be more lively than more compact breeds.

Certain physical characteristics can also be attributed to the cat's place of origin. Cats that have originated in colder climates – especially Northern Europe – have stocky, solid and sturdy bodies, large, rounded heads, moderately short, broad muzzles and short, thick tails. To endure the cold environment, their bodies are structured to retain body heat. The Maine Coon and the Norwegian Forest Cat are good examples of this category.

Semi-foreign breeds that originated in the warmer climates of Africa and Asia are more slender and muscular than their cold-weather counterparts, and are quite elegant, with moderately wedge-shaped heads, oval paws and long, gently tapering tails. On their slender but muscular legs, they stand taller than those cats from colder climates. Semi-foreign breeds

are currently popular with cat breeders, and many of the recently recognized breeds in the world fall into this category. Examples of these cats are the Abyssinian and Turkish Angora. Some of the more recent efforts to create wild-looking cats, such as the Ocicat, use semi-foreign parent breeds and this is reflected in their type.

Oriental breeds, which originated in hot, tropical countries, are the most dramatically slender cats, with long bodies and long, thin tails. To keep the cats cool

BELOW: Oriental cats have an exotic body shape. They are athletic and slender in appearance.

CAT FACT
Cats make up to 20 different sounds.

in the warm climate, their bodies are designed to let heat escape by having the maximum surface area for their size. The Siamese, with its wedge-shaped head and large ears, is a perfect example of this breed. Newer breeds have been created that mimic the Oriental style. The Oriental Shorthair, for example, is the solid-colored version of the Siamese.

Other Western breeds, such as the Cornish and Devon Rexes, have been bred to look rather like Oriental breeds.

BELOW: The Cornish Rex has been selectively bred to mimic the slender body shape of the Oriental breeds.

Eye Shape and Color

Like cats themselves, cats' eyes are exotic and beautiful. These windows of mystery range in color from the golden copper and yellow of the wildcat, to the yellow, green and blue found in domestic breeds. Most eye colors are not governed by coat color. The only exception is white-coated cats with blue eyes. Blue is the eye color of all new-born kittens. Blue eyes lack pigment, allowing more light to enter the eye. This lack of pigmentation affects the color of the coat, too, and occurs in cats with a high degree of white in their coats. Unfortunately, white cats with blue eyes are often deaf because the gene that results in their lack of pigmentation also causes the fluid to dry up in the inner ear soon after birth, preventing the effective transmission of sound waves through to the auditory nerve. Sadly, there is no treatment for this condition. The blue eyes of Siamese cats are not linked to deafness, but may be associated, instead, with poor three-dimensional vision.

The cat's breed may also be indicated by the shape of its eyes. Although most wildcats typically have slanted oval eyes, the eye shapes of domestic cats have been altered through centuries of cross-breeding. Round, prominent eyes can be indicative of the original Western breeds as well as some Eastern, while slanted, almond-shaped eyes are common to Oriental and foreign breeds.

Siamese

European Shorthair

Persian

Oriental

Chapter Three
POPULAR CAT BREEDS

It is only comparatively recently in the history of cats that they have been domesticated, and selective breeding is still in its relative infancy. As a result, the range of cat breeds is quite small when compared with dogs, and domestic cats still – with a few exceptions, such as the Sphynx – very much resemble their wild ancestors. There is also much less diversity between the different breeds compared with dogs. One of the main reasons, for example, that different cat breeds are broadly of similar size, is the fact that the African Wildcat – ancestor of today's domestic cat breeds – does not vary significantly in size throughout its range. On the other hand, the Gray Wolf – which is the original ancestor of the domestic dog – varies hugely in size across its range and, therefore, domestic dogs vary greatly in size, too.

BELOW: The Sphynx is one of the breeds that bears little resemblance to its wild ancestors.

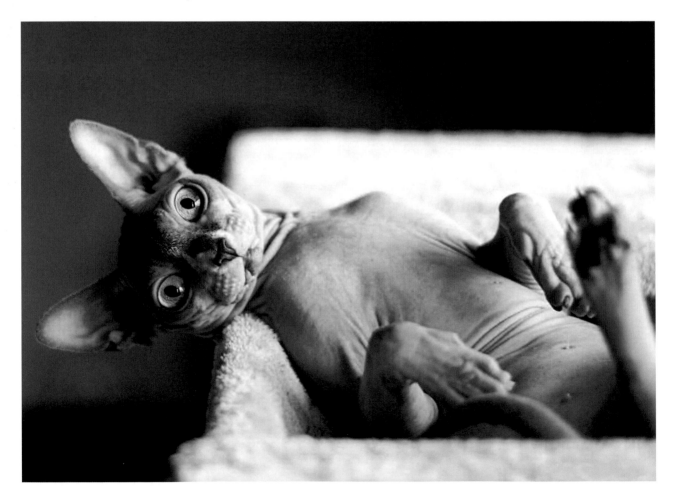

Hybridization

Thanks to advances in DNA technology, studies of the domestic cat's genetic history are now a reality, and so it may become possible in the future to confirm the origins of breeds, as well as their relationships to each other. What is already evident is that, until very recently, there was no other input into their genetic development than from the African Wildcat. It is now considered possible that the longhaired gene was introduced as a result of natural hybridization between domestic cats roaming free and Pallas' Cat, a species found in Asia. Although interest in wildcat crossings has been sparked in recent years by the huge rise in popularity of the Bengal breed, hybridization between wild species of cat and their domestic relatives is nothing new. As long ago as the late 1800s, cat shows had classes for the offspring of such matings. However, none of these hybrids was subsequently developed into a breed at that stage.

In the USA, a number of breeds are currently being developed from wild cats, but recent restrictions on the keeping of such animals as pets looked as though they might stop this trend and that there would therefore be little scope for developing new breeds by further hybridization. However, the development of new breeds continues apace. It remains to be seen, though, whether any will attain the popularity of the Bengal.

BELOW: The Bengal is the result of hybridization. Its beautiful spotted coat is unique to the breed.

ABYSSINIAN

The Abyssinian cat is a natural breed, meaning that there had been no intervention by human beings in its evolution until it was "discovered" in 1868. The present breed is said to be descended from a cat called Zula, brought to England by Captain Barrett Leonard at the conclusion of the Abyssinian War. There are no verifiable written records tracing early Abyssinians to Zula, but such cats were exhibited at the Crystal Palace

LEFT & ABOVE: The Abyssinian is slim and muscular with a wedge-shaped head. Left is a blue and above is a red or sorrel Abyssinian.

in London in 1871, making it certain that all modern Abyssinians are descended from cats bred in the UK.

The breed's true origins are unclear, but it possibly came from areas that may include Egypt, Abyssinia (now Ethiopia), the west coast of India and islands off the coast of East Africa. This is one of the world's oldest cat breeds, and some claim it is the Nile Valley cat, worshipped by the ancient Egyptians. It certainly bears a close resemblance to the sacred cats carved and painted on Egyptian tombs and frescoes, which portray an elegant feline, with a slim but muscular body and a graceful neck.

Appearance Of medium size, slim and muscular, the head is slightly wedge-shaped and gently curved in profile. The American Abyssinian has a shorter head and a more rounded profile than its European counterpart. The nose is medium-length, the ears large, and the oval eyes are large and expressive. The tail is thick at the base, tapering to the tip.

Coat A soft, silky, fine-textured and medium-length coat. All Abyssinians have unusual ticked coats, with two or three dark bands of color in them. The ticking is also known as agouti, referring to a particular rodent whose hair has similar color-banding down its length.

The earliest Abyssinians also displayed tabby barring on the legs, but this has been removed over the generations by selective breeding, to the extent that the only evident tabby markings are now on the head and the characteristic dark tip to the tail. Abyssinians come in a variety of tabby colors: ruddy, red or sorrel, blue, fawn, black silver, and blue silver.

Characteristics and Temperament
An active, intelligent breed, it can nevertheless be shy and mistrustful of strangers. It is, however, loyal and extremely affectionate toward its owners, though the Abyssinian tends to be more a climber than a lap-sitter. They are athletic and entertaining felines, fond of inventing new games.

BELOW: The Abyssinian bears a resemblance to the sacred cats painted on Egyptian tombs.

AMERICAN BOBTAIL

The breed can be traced to a random-bred bobtail kitten that was adopted from a Native American reservation by a couple from Iowa in the 1960s. The genetic antecedents of the breed remain unclear: however, both Manx and Japanese Bobtail genes may be present, as both completely tailless "rumpies" and cats with shorter tails than normal, as well as individuals with tails of normal length, appear in this breed. The American Bobtail was accepted for registration by the CFA in 2000, but only those cats with actual bobtails can be exhibited. The tail, in this case, should extend down to a point just above the hocks, and no lower.

Appearance A medium-to-large cat, the head is a broad, modified wedge, with a distinctive brow above large, almost almond-shaped eyes. Ears are medium with slightly rounded tips. The body is moderately long and the legs are in proportion with the body. The paws are large and round. The tail should be clearly visible above the back when the cat is alert and is not to exceed the hock in length. The optimum tail is articulate and nearly straight with only the slightest of curves. This cat possesses a unique natural hunting gaze that combines with its body-type to give it the distinctive wild look.

Coat The unique coat comes in both a medium, semi-dense shorthair, and a medium-length longhair that is resilient and resistant to water. The topcoat is harsh, with a soft undercoat that insulates the cat from extremes of temperature. The coat requires little or no special attention.

Characteristics and Temperament
The American Bobtail is an extremely adept hunter, whose instincts are satisfied in its domestic setting by catching flying insects mid-air. These cats also like to stalk their toys and carry them off in their mouths, while many are able to open doors by

BELOW: The American Bobtail has a charming personality. They make wonderful pets, noted for their devotion to their owners.

standing on their hind legs and turning doorknobs with their paws. They bond well with their families and get on well with most dogs. Indeed, they are themselves noted for their dog-like devotion to their owners. They make excellent companions for children being, within reason, relatively tolerant of rough handling. This is a slow-maturing breed that takes two to three years to achieve its full adult type.

BELOW: An American Bobtail kitten.

AMERICAN CURL

In 1981, a stray kitten appeared at a home in California. The householder left food on the porch for it, which it ate, and it adopted the house as its home. This female cat had a long, black, silky coat and very unusual ears that curled back away from the face toward the back and center of the head. Later that year, the cat had a litter of kittens, two of which had the same curled ears. These cats were shown in California in 1983 and the breed is now recognized as such in North America. Curls were also the first breed to be admitted to the championship class as one breed with two coat-lengths. Outcrossing, which has produced a shorthaired Curl, ensures that genetic diversity continues to flourish within the breed. When Curls are born, their ears are straight. In 3 to 5 days they begin to curl back, still in a tight rosebud position, unfurling gradually until permanently "set" at around 16 weeks. The curling causes these cats no apparent discomfort or other problems.

BELOW & RIGHT: American Curls can be of any color or coat-pattern. Their coats are fine, silky, and flowing with minimal undercoat.

Appearance The American Curl is a well-balanced, moderately muscled cat that is slender rather than massively built. The head is a modified wedge, with a rounded muzzle and a firm chin. The ears are moderately large, wide at the base and open, curving back in a smooth arc when viewed from the front and rear. The ear-tips are rounded. The eyes are walnut-shaped and slightly tilted. The paws are medium-sized and rounded. The tail is equal to the length of the body, wide at the base, tapering and plumed.

Coat Both shorthaired and longhaired American Curls have soft, silky coats that lie flat against their bodies. The coat is fine, silky and with minimal undercoat. They are bred in a wide range of colors and patterns.

Characteristics and Temperament The American Curl is an alert and active cat with a gentle, equable disposition.

AMERICAN SHORTHAIR

The American Shorthair is similar to British and European Shorthairs, which are the oldest of the recognized shorthaired breeds. The American Shorthair's origins lie with the domestic cats taken to North America by settlers from Europe, dating back to the 1600s. At the beginning of the 20th century, some American breeders decided to develop their domestic cat's characteristics into a distinctive breed, as had happened in Europe with ordinary indigenous shorthairs. The first litter was from a mating of American and British Shorthairs. It was not until 1965 that the breed's name was changed from Domestic Shorthair to American Shorthair, in line with the names given to British and European Shorthairs.

Appearance A sturdy, medium-to-large cat, with a strong, muscular body, larger in size than an ordinary non-pedigree shorthair. The American Shorthair is not excessively cobby or rangy. The head is large with full cheeks and a square muzzle. The eyes are large, round, set widely apart, and slightly slanted. The legs are strong-boned and the paws firm, full, and rounded with heavy pads. The tail is medium-length and heavy at the base, tapering to a blunt end.

Coat The coat is short, dense, even, and firm in texture, being somewhat heavier and thicker in winter. Grooming is easy, and regular combing is all that is required to keep the coat in good condition.

American Shorthairs come in a wide variety of coat- colors and patterns.

Characteristics and Temperament
The American Shorthair is an easy-going, self-sufficient, no-nonsense cat, its equable temperament making it the ideal family pet. It is bold, intelligent, inquisitive, and active, and prefers to have regular access to an outdoor space. It has proved to be both healthy and hardy, and it gets along well with other cats of different types and with dogs – evidence of its great adaptability. Its similarity to British and European Shorthairs, however, has meant that the popularity of the breed has not spread significantly outside North America.

LEFT & RIGHT: The difference between the American Shorthair and its British counterpart is negligible, although there are slight differences between American and British standards for the breeds.

"I have studied many philosophers and many cats. The wisdom of cats is infinitely superior."
Hippolyte Taine (1828-1893)

BALINESE

Once known as the Longhair Siamese, the Balinese is a silky, longer-haired version of the Siamese. The cat's graceful and lithe build is reminiscent of the temple dancers of the Indonesian island of Bali, in whose honor the breed is named. The long-coated kittens that sometimes appear in litters of Siamese cats were developed into the Balinese in the USA in the 1950s, the new breed being introduced to the UK and Europe in the 1970s.

Appearance The Balinese is of medium build but long-limbed and supple. It has a long, wedge-shaped head, wide between the ears and narrowing to the nose which is long and straight. The cat's most distinctive feature is its almond-shaped, slanted sapphire-blue eyes. The ears are large and pointed and the tail is very long and thin, the hair spread out like a plume.

Coat Since it has no undercoat, the Balinese's long and typically pale-colored and fine topcoat feels exceptionally silky and lies flat to the body. The colorpoint coat can be in a range of colors and patterns. The coat needs regular gentle combing, while the tail should be brushed.

Characteristics and Temperament Not surprisingly, Balinese are similar in temperament to Siamese cats. They love being the center of attention and enjoy being part of the family, amusing people with their acrobatic antics. They are usually affectionate but can at times be aloof.

Colors In the UK, all color varieties are attributed to the Balinese, but in the USA only four colors are recognized as traditional – Seal Point, Blue Point, Chocolate Point, and Lilac Point.

BELOW: The Balinese is similar to the Siamese in looks and stature.

BELOW: The Balinese is aristocratic and dainty in appearance.

BENGAL

The Bengal is the result of the crossing of Asian
Leopard Cats with domestic felines to produce a wild-
looking cat with a docile temperament. A rigid
breeding program was established in the 1980s to
diminish the cat's wild tendencies so it would be
suitable to be a domestic pet. Early crosses were to
non-pedigrees, but when the spotted leopard-like coat
appeared, Bengals were crossed with Egyptian Maus
and Ocicats. This practice is no longer condoned by
most breeders.

Appearance Resembling a wild, spotted Asian
Leopard Cat, the Bengal is large-boned and muscular.
The head is a medium wedge-shape and rather small
compared with the body-size. In profile, the forehead,
with its prominent brow, curves gently to the bridge
of the nose. The nose is large and broad and the eyes
are large and almond-shaped. The ears are small.

Coat Unlike any other domestic cat, the Bengal's
thick, luxuriant coat glitters as if sprinkled with gold
dust, the silky texture being more like a wildcat's pelt
than the fur of a domestic cat. Bengals have been
bred with both spotted and so-called marbled tabby
markings, and there are some that have self-
colored coats.

Characteristics and Temperament A friendly, alert,
curious, and intelligent cat, the Bengal has little fear of
other cats, or any other animal for that matter. Bengals
are not afraid of water; indeed, they like to play with
it, and also with toys. They are great climbers and
love high vantage points.

*RIGHT: The Bengal is reminiscent of a wildcat. To achieve
this breed, hybrids of the Asian Leopard Cat were bred with
domestic cats.*

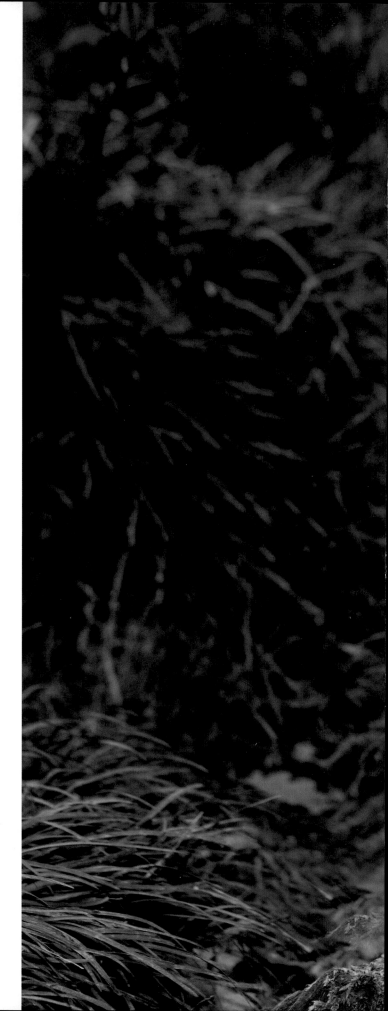

BIRMAN

First bred as a pedigree cat in France in the early 1920s, the beautiful semi-longhaired Birman was slower to gain popularity in the USA and the UK, where it was not recognized until the late 1960s. Various legends attempt to explain the ancestry of the Birman as originating in the temples of Burma (Myanmar). However, the true origins of the breed are as yet unknown.

Appearance The Birman's large body has thickset legs of medium length and short paws that end in distinctive white gloves. The head is broad and rounded, with full cheeks and a strong chin. Eyes are almost round and a deep blue. The tail is medium-length and full. All Birmans have colorpointed features.

Coat The coat is long, silky, and slightly curled on the belly, with a full ruff around the neck. All Birmans are colorpointed, with darker coloration on the ears, face, tail, and legs. As long as it is brushed and combed regularly, the coat is comparatively easy to keep well-groomed and in good condition.

BELOW: Birmans are playful, sociable, and gentle.

Characteristics and Temperament Birmans are proud, intelligent, and inquisitive. They love people and are extremely loyal. Birman kittens are particularly mischievous and their sense of fun stays with them into adulthood. They are also gentle and sensitive, and being sociable animals, will tolerate other pets quite happily. They quickly adapt to new surroundings, but have a tendency to pine if left alone for long periods of time.

Colors The color of the coat is light, preferably with a golden cast, as if misted with gold, while the "points" of the face, legs, and tail are darker, similar to the Siamese, and with colorpointed Persian patterns of Seal, Blue, Chocolate, and Lilac. Eye-color for all varieties is blue.

BELOW: Birmans are famous for their white "socks."

BOMBAY

The Bombay was named in honor of the Indian city of that name, now Mumbai, because of the cat's resemblance to the black panther – a native of India. In the 1950s, an American breeder successfully recreated the look of the wild panther by crossing black American Shorthairs and Sable Burmese, and the breed was first recognized in the mid 1970s. In the UK, black British Shorthairs were mated with Burmese and became part of the Asian Group breeding program.

Appearance The cat has a medium-sized muscular body with a rounded head and a full face. It has a short snub nose and a firm chin. The medium-sized ears have rounded tips and are tilted slightly forward, giving the cat an alert expression. The eyes are large, round, and copper-colored. The legs are in proportion with the body and the paws are round. Everything about the cat is black, from the nose to the paw-pads.

Coat The short coat lies close to the body, with a sheen that gave rise to the cat's nickname in America as "the patent-leather kid with new-penny eyes." The fur must be jet black from root to tip. The coat needs little attention to keep it in excellent condition, but buffing it with a silk scarf or velvet grooming mitt will certainly enhance the natural sheen.

Characteristics and Temperament The Bombay has the typical Burmese temperament to the point of being almost sedate, making it a good pet. But it is also gregarious, affectionate, and requires plenty of attention.

LEFT: The Bombay is a product of the vogue for the wild and exotic that arose in the second half of the 20th century and continues to this day.

BRITISH SHORTHAIR

The breed stems from the first domestic cats that arrived in Britain with the Romans in the 1st century AD. The modern breed was developed in the 1880s from farm, street, and domestic cats in the UK, in response to the growing interest in showing cats that had begun by this stage. The breed was in decline by the turn of the 20th century, however, due to the rise in popularity of more exotic breeds for show purposes, notably Persian Longhairs, and had almost died out by the 1950s. At that time, matings with Blue Persians then resulted in the British Shorthairs being developed in terms of their size and appearance, and helped them to regain their popularity. Similar breeding programs over recent years have led to the introduction of new color variants to the breed, such as Chocolate and Lilac, as well as the creation of a Colorpoint lineage which

BELOW: The "British Blue" shorthair was the first of the British Shorthairs. It is a popular variant known for its good nature and even temperament.

combines the markings of the Colorpoint Longhair (Himalayan) breed with the appearance of the British Shorthair. Nowadays, the British Shorthair has become the third largest group of registered pedigree cats in the UK, thanks partly to the exposure which the breed has received as a result of its use in various advertising campaigns for cat food.

Appearance The Shorthair's compact, well- balanced and powerful body makes it deceptively heavy. The chest is full and broad, legs are short and strong with large, rounded paws, and the tail is thick at the base and rounded at the tip. The head is very broad and round with well-developed cheeks. The eyes are large and round, while the ears are small and neat.

Coat The coat is short, thick and fine. Numerous guard hairs give the coat its distinctive, crisp texture, while the protective undercoat insulates the cat from the cold. Daily grooming with a comb helps keep the coat in prime condition, although unlike the Longhair, this is not essential.

British Shorthairs come in a wide variety of coat-colors and patterns.

Characteristics and Temperament
Its intelligent yet phlegmatic nature makes the British Shorthair a solid and dependable feline companion that responds readily to affection. It is also self-possessed and self-reliant, undemanding yet friendly. The breed may appear to be a cuddly cross between a cat and a teddy bear, but they are also skilled hunters, and toms can be determined

fighters due to their strongly developed territorial instincts. Neutering helps modify these aggressive tendencies toward other cats, but should not be carried out too early, before the distinctive fleshy pads, called jowls, have developed around the face. This creates what has been likened to a double-chinned appearance, which would otherwise not appear, as they are only seen in mature males.

RIGHT: British Shorthairs have long been prized for their physical strength and hunting ability. For many years they were considered to be working cats.

BURMESE

In 1930, a Siamese hybrid female, named Wong Mau, was brought from Rangoon in Burma (Myanmar) to the USA and mated with a Seal-Point Siamese. Some of the resulting offspring were dark brown and formed the beginnings of the official pedigree Burmese. The breed was registered in 1936, and was eventually recognized in the UK in 1952. Since then, the breed has developed to slightly different standards on opposite sides of the Atlantic, with the result that there are now different classes at many cat shows in North America, catering separately for Burmese but also Burmese of European appearance.

Appearance Despite having genetic material almost identical to that of the Siamese, the Burmese is rather more compactly built, in that it was subsequently evolved along less extreme lines. In fact, these cats approximate more closely in type to the early Siamese, compared with their contemporary cousins. The nose has an obvious break in its line, the head

LEFT: Burmese are commonly bred in two types: traditional and contemporary, the latter having a more rounded look as the cat pictured here.

being round with very full cheeks. The eyes are large, round and yellow-to-gold in color. The cats have well-proportioned legs and neat, oval paws. The tail is straight and of medium length, tapering to a rounded tip. Burmese of US origin are more stocky in form, a fact emphasized by their legs, which are slightly shorter than those of their European counterparts; these have a more angular profile overall, together with oval-shaped eyes.

Coat The short, fine, silky coat is close-lying and needs very little grooming to keep it in top condition.

Burmese come in a wide variety of coat-colors and patterns.

THE CAT

William Henry Davies (1871-1940)

Within that porch, across the way,
I see two naked eyes this night;
Two eyes that neither shut nor blink,
Searching my face with a green light.

But cats to me are strange, so strange —
I cannot sleep if one is near;
And though I'm sure I see those eyes,
I'm not so sure a body's there!

"The smallest feline is a masterpiece."
Leonardo da Vinci (1452-1519)

BURMILLA

An accidental mating in 1981 between a Lilac Burmese female and a Chinchilla Silver male resulted in the birth of attractive shaded-silver female kittens. They were all of a shorthaired Burmese type with the tipping and outlined features of the Chinchilla. Similar matings were carried out and in 1983 the Cat Association of Great Britain accepted breeding programs and a standard of points for the breed to be known as the Burmilla. Kittens are paler in color than adults, while Shaded varieties have darker coats than Tipped varieties.

Appearance The female Burmilla is markedly smaller and daintier than the male, but the body type is generally medium-sized and straight-backed. Legs are long and sturdy with neat, oval paws. The Burmilla carries its tail high and proud. The head is a medium wedge, gently rounded at the top, and the ears are large. The large, expressive eyes are outlined with dark "eyeliner," while the lips and nose-leather are similarly outlined. The tail is medium-to-long, fairly thick at the base, and tapering slightly to a rounded tip.

Coat The coat is short, dense, soft and glossy, slightly longer than that of the Burmese and with enough undercoat to give it a slight lift. The Burmilla's most impressive feature is the sparkling shading or tipping on its coat. It is best to groom the dense coat with a rubber brush, so that dead hairs can be loosened first before combing them out.

Characteristics and Temperament
The Burmilla is stable and dignified but inquisitive and sociable, too, though less boisterous than the typical Burmese. It is playful and very affectionate.

LEFT: The Burmilla's eyes are clear and bright and can come in any shade of green, although amber eyes are acceptable in Red, Creams, and Torties.

CHARTREUX

Origins Native to France, this breed is said to have been bred as long ago as the 16th century near the French city of Grenoble, at the Monastery of La Grande Chartreuse (which was also responsible for the liqueur of that name). The Chartreux is not bred in many European countries, but it was first brought to the US in 1971 by Helen and John Gammon of La Jolla, California, although there are fewer than two dozen active Chartreux breeders in North America as of 2007. This breed should not be confused with the British Blue or the European Shorthair Blue.

Appearance Well-proportioned but stocky, with short legs and large, muscular shoulders, the Chartreux is rather lighter than its counterpart, the British Blue. Its head is large and round with well-developed cheeks and a short, strong neck. Eyes are large and open, not too rounded and with the outer corners slightly uptilted. Eye-color is a vivid deep yellow to a vivid deep copper. Ears are medium-sized and set high on the head. Paws are large and the tail is medium-length with a rounded tip.

Coat The coat is dense, soft, and plush with a slightly woolly undercoat and a glossy appearance. Daily grooming with a comb is needed to keep the undercoat in good condition, while brushing enhances the way in which the coat characteristically stands away from the body.

Characteristics and Temperament
A calm, affectionate, intelligent and attentive cat. It is less talkative than most breeds, having a high-pitched meow and an infrequently used chirp. It will happily live confined to the house, making it a suitable pet for an apartment-dweller.

CAT FACT

Legend has it that the Chartreux's ancestors may have been feral mountain cats from what is now Syria, brought back to France by returning Crusaders in the 13th century, many of whom entered the Carthusian monastic order.

LEFT & RIGHT: The Chartreux is famous for its incredible amber eyes and gray coat.

CORNISH REX

The first recorded Cornish Rex kitten was born in 1950 in Cornwall, England. The kitten, named Kallibunker, was red with a white chest and belly and its fur was closely waved. It was mated with its mother, and the resulting litter contained two curly-coated kittens. Descendants were then backcrossed to Rex cats to create the recessive curly coat. The breed was officially recognized in 1967 in the UK and in 1979 in the USA.

Appearance The Cornish Rex is medium-sized, hard-bodied, muscular, and slender, with a curving back and huge ears set high on a disproportionately small head. The body, with its arched back, is set on fine, slender legs. The American standard requires a "tucked-up" torso that gives the cat the appearance of a whippet, a breed of dog. Eyes are oval and medium-to-large in size, being a full eye's width apart and slanting slightly upward. Eye-color is clear and intense and corresponds with the coat-color for the breed standard. It includes eyes that are blue, gold, green, and hazel, while some cats are odd-eyed.

Coat The Cornish Rex's most unusual feature is its short, plush, coat, characterized by a relatively dense, tight, washboard wave, lying close to the body and extending from the top of the head across the back, sides, flanks and tail. Because it is lacking in guard hairs, the cat's single downy undercoat is soft and velvety to the touch. Hair is shed very gradually, rather as in the case of a human being, thus making grooming simple.

Cornish Rexes comes in a wide variety of coat-colors and patterns.

LEFT & RIGHT: The Cornish Rex is the result of a natural mutation. It is bred to duplicate the recessive gene responsible for its distinctive curly coat.

Characteristics and Temperament
Affectionate and people-oriented, the Cornish Rex wags its tail to show it is happy. Lively, playful, and agile, it is capable of leaping effortlessly from ground to shoulder height. It enjoys games of fetch and catch and likes to bat at objects with its paws.

DEVON REX

In 1960, in Devon, England, a curly-coated feral male was mated with a stray, straight-haired female. The litter included one curly-coated male, named Kirlee, demonstrating that the curly hair gene was recessive. The parents were almost certainly related, and inbreeding was required to perpetuate the breed. By 1970, the Devon Rex had been recognized in the UK, but it was not until 1979 that it was accepted in the USA.

Appearance The Devon Rex shares the muscular build, slim legs, and long, whip-like tail of the Cornish Rex; however, it is broad-chested, and has a flat forehead, prominent cheekbones, and a crinkled brow. Its coat runs in a rippled pattern rather than being wavy like the Cornish Rex, which is a quite separate mutation in spite of both breeds having arisen in neighboring counties in the south-west of England. The face of the Devon Rex is wide with large, round eyes, prominent, brittle whiskers, and huge, low-set ears. They are commonly nicknamed "poodle cats" because of their coats and habit of wagging their tails. The cats have quizzical, impish expressions that evoke "extraterrestrials."

Coat The Devon Rex coat is generally less dense and coarser and curlier than that of the Cornish Rex and, without careful breeding, very sparse coats can result. Kittens, in particular, often have relatively thin coats, and even the whiskers are affected and, being crinkled, tend to break more easily than normal.

BELOW & RIGHT: Just like the Cornish Rex, the Devon Rex possesses a curly hair gene.

The coat requires gentle stroking with a soft mitt rather than brushing, and a piece of silk is often favored by exhibitors to give a good gloss to the coat when showing.

All coat-colors, patterns, and color combinations are permitted in the case of this breed.

Characteristics and Temperament

This is certainly a cat for the connoisseur. Even more playful than the Cornish Rex, the Devon Rex loves fooling around and can be extremely mischievous and demanding of human attention, while at the same time being loving and intelligent.

EGYPTIAN MAU

Images of spotted tabby cats can not only be admired in the tomb paintings and scrolls of ancient Egypt, but its descendants may also be seen on the streets of Cairo today. Many believe Egyptian Maus are direct descendants of the African wildcats that they resemble more than any other domestic cat. Maus were probably introduced into Europe aboard the ships of Phoenician traders more than 2,000 years ago. The current stock in the USA is descended from three Maus imported into the country in the 1950s by an exiled Russian princess.

Appearance The Egyptian Mau is medium-sized, long and graceful, with a head that is a slightly rounded wedge-shape. The medium-to-large ears are alert and slightly pointed, and the inner ear is a delicate shell pink. Legs are in proportion with the body and the paws are small and slightly oval. The tail is thick at the base and slightly tapered toward the tip.

Coat The coat is short and silky with random spots that vary in size and shape. The spots form a

contrast to the lighter background coat that comes in just three colors: Silver, Bronze, and Black Smoke. The hair has two or more bands of ticking, separated by lighter bands. The coat is easy to maintain but needs regular grooming.

Characteristics and Temperament

Maus are alert, affectionate, and intelligent but also rather shy, being good with children while disliking strangers. They are happiest when they have sufficient space for jumping, climbing, and hunting.

Colors Of the three traditional color-forms, the Bronze is seemingly the most ancient. Markings on the flanks are random, but spots along the spine run in symmetrical lines, often merging into a dorsal stripe at the root of the tail.

BELOW: The Egyptian Mau is an elegant and beautiful cat.

ABOVE: The Egyptian Mau as it is today was essentially bred and developed in the USA.

EUROPEAN SHORTHAIR

The first European Shorthairs were descended from cats introduced to Northern Europe nearly 2,000 years ago by Roman soldiers, who brought the cats with them to control rodents in their food stores. Until 1982, European Shorthairs were classified with British Shorthairs. FIFe then gave the breed its own category and it developed effectively as a ready-made breed, with a full range of colors, established types, and with breeding-stock with known histories. The cat is now being selectively bred, this trend having begun in Scandinavia. Today, British Shorthair crosses are excluded from the pedigree of European Longhairs, as are Persian Longhairs, used in the past to increase

the size of the British breed. The European Longhair is not recognized by the GCCF or other major breed registries outside of Europe.

Appearance More elegant than the British Shorthair, emphasis in the European Shorthair lies in its lithe muscularity rather than rounded cobbiness. Its face is slightly longer and less heavily jowled than that of its British cousin, while the body is strong and broad-chested, with fairly long, well-boned legs, and firm, rounded paws. The tail is in proportion

BELOW & RIGHT: European Shorthairs are hardy and long-lived. They enjoy being outdoors, so don't do well when confined.

with the body and rounded at the tip. The largish ears, with their rounded tips, are pricked and set fairly widely apart. The eyes are large, round, and well-spaced.

Coat The all-weather coat, which stands away from the body, is short and dense with a crisp texture. Grooming is a simple matter, and regular brushing to keep the undercoat in good condition is all that is necessary. European Shorthairs come in a wide variety of coat-colors and patterns.

Characteristics and Temperament
Being particularly adaptable, independent and intelligent, the cat must not be confined indoors. It is placid and affectionate, making it an ideal family pet.

EXOTIC SHORTHAIR

The breed was developed in the mid 1960s, the aim being to produce a shorthaired Persian cat. Persians were thus crossed with various shorthairs and the product was a shorthaired cat that required minimal grooming and had the Persian's gentle nature. It also has all the physical characteristics of the Persian cat, and is available in the same colors and variations. Some Exotic Shorthairs have also inherited the defects of the Persians, so that in North America only outcrosses between American Shorthairs and Persians are permitted. Elsewhere, other breeds may on occasions be used.

Appearance The Exotic Shorthair is of a medium-to-large cobby build. The head is round and massive and set on a short, thick neck. The cat has full cheeks and broad, powerful jaws. The eyes are large, round, and bright. The nose is short and stubby, and the ears are small and blunt, set widely apart and leaning slightly forward.

Coat The coat can neither be called short nor is it semi-long; in fact, it is slightly longer than that of other shorthairs while not being long enough to actually flow. The texture, being neither flat nor close-lying, is dense, plush, soft, and lively. Known as "the lazy man's Persian," grooming is an easier matter, but brushing and combing is necessary a few times a week; shiny fur is achieved by correct feeding. The coat occurs in all colors found in American Shorthairs and Persians.

Exotic Shorthairs come in a wide variety of coat-colors and patterns.

Characteristics and Temperament
The Exotic Shorthair has the placidity and dignity of the Persian yet has a playful and affectionate side to its nature. It is patient with children and is content to be an indoor cat.

LEFT & RIGHT: The Exotic Shorthair is a hardy and robust breed, not reaching maturity until the age of two.

LEFT & RIGHT: *Havana Browns are famous for their rich brown coats. They are very rare and so considered an endangered breed.*

HAVANA BROWN

Breeders had been trying to develop an all-brown cat for 100 years until, in the 1950s, British cat-breeders developed a chestnut (chocolate)-colored cat of Siamese type from the accidental mating of a black non-pedigree cat and a Chocolate-Point Siamese. The unusual name of Havana was chosen because of the striking similarity between the color of these cats and that of the rabbit breed of the same name, although the breed was registered in the UK as the Chestnut Brown Foreign Shorthair, under which name it was known until the 1970s. Havana Browns were also exported to the US, and once American breeders started to develop and raise these cats the UK and US varieties began to assume different characteristics. In England, the Havana has followed the Siamese type by breeding back to the Siamese, and "brown" has been dropped from the breed name. In North America, the breed has retained the original look of the early imports, and the basic genetic theory that produced the Havana Brown has been re-applied to produce the wide range of Oriental solid colors.

Appearance The head is shaped like that of the Siamese, being longer than it is wide. The ears are large and round and slightly pricked to give an alert appearance. The oval eyes are a vivid green. The body is medium-sized, firm and muscular and the medium-length tail tapers gently to a slightly pointed tip. The males are usually larger than the females. All Havana Browns are a warm chestnut-brown color. There is now a distinct difference in appearance between these cats in North America and Europe, with those of North American origins having a less extreme appearance, with a more rounded head-shape than their European counterparts. This is because Siamese have not played such a significant role in their development.

Coat The coat is short-to-medium in length, smooth and lustrous, making it easy to maintain. Combing the coat is sufficient to remove loose hairs.

Characteristics and Temperament
Highly playful, athletic, and energetic animals, Havanas are fond of games and are excellent climbers. These are sweet-tempered and sociable cats, that respond to plenty of attention. They are highly intelligent, and have the unusual habit of using their paws to investigate strange objects by touch, instead of relying on their sense of smell, as is the case with most other breeds.

JAPANESE BOBTAIL

The Japanese Bobtail has existed in Japan for many centuries, where it is considered to be a symbol of domestic good fortune. It probably stemmed from domesticated shorthaired cats that had mutated into tailless versions, and it was not until after the Second World War that the Bobtail was discovered by the international cat-fancying world. In 1963, American judges, visiting a show in Japan, spotted a Bobtail and were impressed. Five years later, an American breeder took 38 Bobtails back to the US and the breed became acceptable for show purposes by the CFA in 1976. The breed is now also recognized in the UK, but is virtually unknown there at present.

Appearance The Japanese Bobtail's distinctive tail is just 3–4-in (8–10-cm) long. It is normally curled up in a bob, but can be held upright when the cat is alert or advertising its presence. The body is medium-sized, slim but well-muscled. The head is pointed, with high cheekbones and slanted eyes that produce a unique profile. It is available in most colors and patterns. In Japan, the Van-patterned Tortie-and-White, known as *Mi-ke* (meaning three colors of black, white, and red), is the most highly prized. There is also a long-coated version of this breed, which was recognized separately from its short-coated counterpart in the USA during 1991. These particular cats appear to be naturally more common in northern parts of Japan, where their tails bear a resemblance to fluffy pompoms.

Coat The coat is medium in length, soft, and silky with no undercoat. Shedding of the hair is slight, and regular combing is all that is required.

Characteristics and Temperament
Bobtails are friendly, curious, and playful, and being very people-oriented make ideal family pets. They have the endearing habit of raising a paw as if in greeting, and this image can be seen all over Japan, translated to ceramic figurines. Bobtails also have soft voices, and use a range of different sounds. They enjoy swimming and can easily be taught to retrieve objects, being masters of the pounce. They love to ride on shoulders, are good travelers, and quickly adjust to dogs and other animals.

CAT FACT

It is apparent from written records that the domestic cat first arrived in Japan from China or Korea at least 1,000 years ago.

ABOVE: The Japanese Bobtail has existed in Japan for centuries. It is often featured in ancient artworks.

LAPERM

In 1986, on a farm in Oregon, a litter of six kittens was born to a domestic cat. One of the kittens was born bald, but within eight weeks had begun to grow soft hair, and by four months had a full coat of wavy hair. It was later mated, and eventually gave birth to five male kittens, all bald at birth as their mother had been. Not being very knowledgeable about cats, the owner accepted the spontaneous "mutant" as unique and thought nothing more of the matter, but the breed turned out to be genetically unique and unrelated to any other Rex variety, the dominant gene having brought about the curious coat. The owner gave the cats the breed name "LaPerm," signifying a wavy or rippled coat. The LaPerm Society of America (LPSA) was formed in 1997 and became affiliated to the CFA, helping to promote the

RIGHT: Many LaPerm owners give their cats Native American names because the breed first occurred in the sacred territory of the Wishram people, a Chinookan-speaking tribe.

breed in that organization. The majority of LaPerms being shown in both TICA and CFA events are in the USA, although the UK now has a large LaPerm breeding program, and is the home of the LaPerm Cat Club. The breed has made solid progress within the GCCF and is often seen at British cat shows. In June 2008 a LaPerm gained provisional recognition in the GCCF and was the first to gain an Intermediate Certificate.

Appearance The face and head is somewhat triangular in shape, the ears set widely apart. Whisker-pads are relatively large, and eyes are large and expressive. LaPerms can also boast a splendid set of curly whiskers and eyebrows.

Coat The coat forms waves or ringlets that range from tight to long corkscrew curls, depending on whether the cat is short- or long-coated. The coat generally stands away from the body, parting down the center. Grooming is minimal because the coat does not easily mat. Because of the appearance of its coat, the breed is still sometimes known as the Alpaca Cat, the alpaca being a relative of the shaggy-coated llama, highly prized for the quality of its wool.

Characteristics and Temperament
LaPerms are gentle and affectionate but also very active. But unlike many energetic breeds, they are also content to be lap cats. They positively seek out human contact and will purr as soon as they see you, making them possibly the most sociable breed of all. They are generally quiet animals, but can become more vocal when clamoring for attention.

MAINE COON

This is one of the oldest natural breeds in North America and has been recognized as a true variety for well over 100 years. The breed originated in the state of Maine on the north-eastern side of the USA. The name "coon"' arose because the cat was once believed to be the product of matings between domestic cats and racoons – although this is not biologically possible. A more romantic theory suggests that Queen Marie-Antoinette sent her cats to America during the time of the French Revolution, and these became the ancestors of the breed. The more likely explanation is that the Maine Coon resulted from matings between domestic Shorthairs, introduced by early settlers, and Angora types later transported across the Atlantic Ocean by seafarers. A Maine Coon won the Best in Show award at the 1895 Madison Square Garden Show, but the breed did not achieve wide international recognition until the 1980s. In fact, it faded from the cat scene in its homeland in the early 1900s, as breeders preferred to show more exotic cats, such as Persian Longhairs, which, at this stage, had been introduced to the USA from Europe.

Appearance A handsome, sturdy, medium-to-large cat. The head has a gently concave outline when viewed in profile, with a squared-off muzzle. The nose is of medium length. Eyes are large and slightly oval, with eye-color ranging from green, blue, and hazel to copper. The large ears are wide at the base and set well apart on the head. The tips of the ears bear small tufts of fur. The Maine Coon has a long,

PAGES 70-71: The Maine Coon is a large rugged animal with a water-resistant coat and a hardy constitution.

muscular and well-proportioned body with medium-length legs and large, round paws. The impressive tail should be nearly as long as the body.

Coat These are semi-longhaired cats with heavy, shaggy fur which tends to be thicker and longer around the back, sides and belly. There should also be a full frill around the neck, although this is lost when much of the longer hair is molted in the spring, being a feature associated with the winter coat. The fur on the tail should be long and flowing. Many colors are recognized in the breed, and tabby patterns are particularly common.

Characteristics and Temperament

Although large, these cats are sweet-natured, friendly creatures. Both attractive and amusing in their antics, they are considered by many to be the ideal pet cat. They are slow to mature and may take up to four years to attain full adult stature. Due to their above-average intelligence, Maine Coons are known to be one of the easiest felines to train.

Typical Maine Coon Varieties:

The coat must be solid to the roots and free from shadings, markings or hair of another color. Patterning should cover the coat, including the legs and tail in Tortoiseshells. In Bi-Colors and Parti-Colors, any solid, Tortoiseshell, Tabby, Shaded, or Smoke color, combined with white, is acceptable.

MANX

This unusual, tailless cat hails from the Isle of Man, UK. The lack of a tail, however, is a genetic mutation that occurs occasionally in all animals. In isolated populations, and islands are a good example, there is a greater chance that such a gene will be perpetuated. The original mutation must have occurred many years ago, for Manx cats had been known for a long time to a specialist breed club first established in the UK in 1901. Although it is an old breed, Manx cats remain rare. Breeders have to cross tailless Manx with Manx that have tails, there being a lethal genetic factor involved in tailless-to-tailless pairings which will cause some of the kittens to die at or shortly after birth.

Appearance The breed's most obvious characteristic is its frequent lack of a tail and its rounded body shape. The only acceptable form for showing is the Rumpy, on whose rump there is a slight hollow where the tail should be. There are also three recognized varieties with residual tails of varying lengths: the Rumpy Riser has only a vestigial knob for a tail, the Stumpy has a short tail, while the Longy has a shortened but otherwise normal tail. Manx cats also have a distinctive "bunny-hop" gait, caused by the lack of a tail combined with hind legs that are longer than the front legs.

Coat There are two types of Manx coats, Shorthair and Longhair (formerly Cymric), the coat-length being the only difference between the two. The

Shorthair has a double coat, the outer guard hairs of which are somewhat harsh but glossy in appearance. A softer coat may occur in Whites and Dilutes, where the coat is short, dense and double, giving it a padded quality due to the comparatively long, open, topcoat and the close, cottony undercoat. The Longhair has a silky texture to its coat, which is of medium length, the britches, abdomen, and neck-ruff being longer than the coat on the main body, with tufts of fur between the toes and full ear furnishings. The silky texture is soft, and lies smoothly on the body, while at the same time is full and plush due to the double coat. Regular grooming is essential. Manx cats come in a variety of coat-colors and patterns.

Characteristics and Temperament

The Manx is a playful cat, as a rule, and is an excellent jumper, helped by its powerful hind quarters; it is not unusual to find it perching on the highest point in any room. Many exhibit dog-like characteristics, such as retrieving and burying their toys. Some seem to bond only with a particular person, while others could be described as family pets and will readily accept attention from any human source. Once the former type of bond has been established, however, it may be difficult for many Manx cats to be happy in a different home.

LEFT & BELOW: The Manx is a breed of cat which has a natural mutation to its spine which effects whether it is born with or without a tail.

NORWEGIAN FOREST CAT

Although its origins are unknown, it is possible that the Norwegian Forest Cat can trace its ancestry back to longhaired Turkish cats, which had arrived in Norway by around AD 1000 with Viking traders from the East. For centuries, the "Wegie" was used as a working cat on Scandinavian farms, but it was not until the 1930s that it was taken seriously as a breed, although planned breeding did not begin until the 1970s. The first Wegies arrived in the US in 1979 and in the UK in the 1980s, since when the breed has established a strong international following.

Appearance The long, strongly-built body and long hind legs give the Wegie a solid bearing. The cat's head is triangular with a long, straight profile, and the ears are pointed and erect. The eyes are large and open and the chin is firm. The tail is long and bushy and the paws are tufted.

Coat The Wegie's double-layered coat grows heavier during winter to keep out the cold and wet. A woolly undercoat keeps the body warm, while a smooth, water-repellent topcoat keeps out rain and snow. The generous frill of fur at the neck and chest is

likely to be shed during the warmer summer months.

Wegies come in a wide variety of coat-colors and patterns.

Characteristics and Temperament

The Wegie is generally active and alert. It can be very playful while retaining the independent character of its semi-wild forbears. It is affectionate but dislikes being cosseted and will defend its territory vigorously. It is a superb climber and hunter, and has even been known to fish in streams. This cat must not be confined indoors.

Typical Norwegian Forest Cat Varieties

In these cats there is no relationship between coat-color and eye-color, as is the case in most other pedigree breeds.

RIGHT: The Wegie is a very old breed from Norway, where it has featured in legends and folktales for hundreds of years.

RIGHT: *Wegies have dense water-repellent coats that help them withstand the harsh winters of Scandinavia.*

OCICAT

The first offspring of this breed appeared in the 1960s as the result of an accidental mating of a hybrid Abyssinian-Siamese female with a Chocolate-Point Siamese male. The spotted pattern of the kitten reminded its breeder's daughter of a baby ocelot, and she decided to produce similar cats which were eventually recognized as a separate breed. Now named the Ocicat, it obtained full championship status in North America in 1987. A similar breeding program has seen the Ocicat being created along similar lines in Europe, where it is currently increasing in popularity.

Appearance The Ocicat is a rather large but well-proportioned cat, being powerful and agile with a typical "wildcat" appearance. The head is wedge-shaped with clear and definite markings that include the characteristic tabby M on the forehead. It has a broad muzzle and strong chin, the ears being large and pricked. The Ocicat is remarkable for its striking, almond-shaped eyes. The long body is athletic and muscular, the legs are long, and the tail is fairly long and slightly tapered.

Coat The Ocicat's coat is short and smooth, satiny and lustrous. All hairs, except those on the tip of the tail, are banded. The hairs of the base color are tipped with a lighter color. The pattern is that of a Spotted Tabby, though the spotted patterning becomes less obvious during a molt. The tail should always end in a dark tip, reflecting the true coat-color of the individual. Gentle brushing is all that is required by way of grooming. Originally, the number of Ocicat colors was restricted, but more were introduced by crossing examples of the breed with American Shorthairs. The range of colors now includes Chocolate, Blue, Lavender, and Fawn, as well as Silver and Smoke variants.

Characteristics and Temperament

Ocicats are loving and gentle, inquisitive and playful, and make excellent pets, being outgoing and friendly toward strangers and even dogs. They enjoy exploring their surroundings and need to be given plenty of opportunity to climb trees.

BELOW & RIGHT: The Ocicat has been bred to look like a domesticated version of a jungle cat.

ORIENTAL SHORTHAIR

Oriental cats first became popular in the early 1960s when a small number of breeders began mating Siamese with indigenous cats, such as the British, European and American Shorthairs, to produce a wide range of colors and patterns. They have since only been outcrossed to Siamese. The care taken with the selection of their foundation stock ensures strength, stamina and good temperament, as well as beauty. This is one of the most diverse of all cat breeds and groups.

Appearance By and large, Oriental cats are identical to Siamese cats in all respects except for having all-over coat-color and pattern rather than the Siamese colorpoints on face, ears, tail, and legs. Unlike the Siamese, most Orientals do not have blue eyes. Their appearance is almost canine – moving as they do like whippets – while swishing a whip-like tail.

Coat The Oriental cat's coat has a short, fine texture that is glossy and close-lying. They are naturally very clean cats and minimal grooming is required, but buffing the coat with a soft glove or silk scarf is recommended to bring out the gloss.

Characteristics and Temperament

This is an extrovert cat, intelligent, inquisitive, and very affectionate. It is active and playful and detests being left alone for long periods. The Oriental is as talkative as the Siamese but its voice is a little quieter. Many people find that its response to humans is much like that of a dog, in that Orientals will often run to greet their owners on their return home, demanding to be played with.

Coat Orientals come in many colors including: White, Black, Blue, Chocolate, Lilac, Cinnamon, Caramel, Fawn, Red Self, and Cream. Also varieties of Tortie, Tabby and Smokes, Shaded and Tipped.

PAGES 78-79: Orientals, despite their svelte and graceful lines, are surprisingly weighty and muscular. They are neither frail nor fragile.

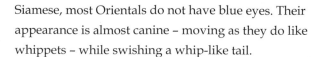

PERSIAN

The true longhaired cat is the Persian, also known as the Longhair or Persian Longhair. The breed probably occurred through matings between Angora cats, which came from the Ankara region of Turkey, and others from Persia (now Iran). It is said that the first examples of these longhaired cats reached Italy and France in the 17th century, but it wasn't until the middle of the 19th century that they acquired pedigree status. Today, Persian cats occur in a staggering variety of colors and patterns.

The typical Persian cat has a luxuriant, silky coat that consists of long guard hairs and shorter down hairs. Unfortunately, because of the nature of their coats, even the most fastidious self-groomer will still need daily attention from its owner. If you are thinking of acquiring a Longhair, the time needed for such regular grooming must be taken into consideration, as well as the fact that, the cats being year-round molters, your carpets, clothes, and furniture will also become liberally covered with their hairs. There is no denying, however, the extraordinary presence of the Persian cat, added to which is its placid, friendly though somewhat detached temperament.

Appearance The body is massive and powerful, with a short neck, a broad chest, and short, stocky legs. The paws are large and round and may be tufted. The head is large and round, with small, round-tipped ears and a short, broad nose. The eyes are large, round, and set wide apart. The tail is short but very full, in keeping with the luxuriant coat.

Coat The Persian has a full and flowing coat of long, dense fur that tangles easily and needs daily brushing and combing to prevent matting. The fur around the neck is extra-long, forming the typical ruff. Persians come is a huge variety of coat and eye color.

Characteristics and Temperament
Quiet and affectionate, though somewhat detached, the Persian is ideally suited to life in an apartment, in that it prefers to be indoors, although it may equally enjoy outdoor life. It is the breed most likely to accept other cats into its home. As kittens, Persians are playful and mischievous.

LEFT: The Persian's ancestors were imported from Persia into Italy in 1620 by Pietro della Valle, and from Turkey into France by Nicolas-Claude Fabri de Peiresc at about the same time, reaching Britain soon after, where they gained popularity with the Royal Family.

RAGDOLL

The world's largest domestic feline, the Ragdoll is a
relatively new breed. Originating in California, the
first steps towards creating it were rather muddled. A
mitted Seal-Point Birman male was mated with a non-
pedigree longhaired white female, and the resulting
semi-longhaired kittens were cross-bred to produce
the first pedigree Ragdolls. The original breeder
coined the name Ragdoll because of the cat's
tendency to go limp in people's arms. The Ragdoll has
become a firm favorite in the USA and has also been
exported to Europe and Australasia.

Appearance The Ragdoll has a large build, with a
medium-to-large head, the full cheeks tapering to a
well-developed muzzle. The ears are medium-sized
with rounded tips, and the eyes are large and oval.
The body is long and muscular, with legs of a
proportionate length, ending in large, rounded
paws. The tail is long and bushy.

Coat The coat is semi-long, shorter around the head
and longer toward the tail. The soft, silky texture
makes the coat less prone to matting than the fur of
many longhairs, and needs only moderate grooming.
The coat is dark compared with that of other pointed
breeds. Ragdolls come in a variety of color points
from pale lilac to darkest seal.

Characteristics and Temperament
Ragdolls make good indoor pets, due to their placid
natures. They don't need much exercise and are good
news for wildlife-lovers in that they show little
interest in hunting. However, they are alert,
intelligent and respond well to training. They love
family life and get on well with children. They will
also tolerate being picked up and carried around –
just like a ragdoll, in fact.

*RIGHT: Ragdolls have a trusting nature, so steps should be
taken to protect them from danger.*

RAGAMUFFIN

Ragamuffins are closely associated with their ancestors, the Ragdolls. They were bred specifically for their equable and affectionate temperament and were designated as a separate breed in 1994. While Ragdolls are recognized for competition only in limited colors, the Ragamuffin is permitted in many colors, including all colorpointed varieties.

Appearance The head is a medium-sized, broad, modified wedge. The nose is medium and the eyes are large, oval, expressive, and inquisitive. Ears are medium-sized, with a slight forward tilt and rounded tips. The very large body is heavy, firm, and muscular with a full chest. The tail is long and fluffy, with a slight taper, and is carried higher than the back.

Coat The coat is luxuriously long or semi-long, plush, and silky and shorter on the face. The coat-length varies slightly, but in general is low-maintenance compared with that of other semi-longhaired breeds.

Characteristics and Temperament
Ragamuffins make ideal pets for the first-time cat-owner. They are one of the most relaxed, perfectly happy cats you are ever likely to encounter, with an unusually docile and warm disposition. They are true people-loving cats and get along well with children and other pets, and they love to be where the action is. They also tend to be soft-pawed, rarely uncovering their claws. The Ragamuffin is suitable only as an indoor pet, in that they are without the defense instincts of most other cats and so need to be protected.

Typical Colors All varieties of point colors: red, tortie, mink, sepia, seal, blue, chocolate or lilac; all mink and sepia colors; all colors of Persians in solids, mitted, and parti-colors. There are many colors/patterns available, including Selfs, Tabbies, Torties, and Blue-eyed pointed varieties.

LEFT & BELOW: The Ragamuffin has a personality more like a dog than a cat. They have soft rabbit-like fur and are much larger than most cats.

RUSSIAN BLUE

Legend has it that the Russian Blue is a descendant of ships' cats, brought to Europe in the 1800s from the White Sea area of northern Russia. The modern Russian Blue has bloodlines derived in part from British Blues and from Blue-Point Siamese, consequences of Swedish and British efforts to revive

the breed in the 1950s, following its near extinction during the Second World War. Blue was the original coat-color, and is preferred by traditionalists, but black and white coats are also available, especially in Europe and New Zealand.

Appearance The Russian Blue is of medium size, with a body that is well- muscled but finer-boned than other Shorthairs. The legs are long and the tail is of medium length and thickness. The head is wedge-shaped with a nose of medium length and a level chin. The ears are large and pointed with very little hair inside or out. The eyes are large, almond-shaped, widely-spaced, and a vivid green in color.

Coat The soft, dense, insulating double coat is thick and lustrous, its density causing the coat to stand out from the body. Some breeders say the coat looks best if it is never brushed.

Characteristics and Temperament

A cautious cat, the Russian Blue dislikes changes in its environment and is shy with strangers. A gentle breed, it is among the least destructive of all cats, and is considered by many cat fanciers to be the ideal companion. It is the perfect cat for apartment-dwellers.

CAT FACT

Interestingly, cats use the meow sound to communicate with humans. They do not use the meow to communicate with other cats.

LEFT & RIGHT: The Russian Blue used to be known as the Archangel Cat, or Foreign Blue.

BELOW & RIGHT: Savannahs are one of the larger breeds of domestic cat, their actual weight being deceptively heavy, given their tall, slim build.

SAVANNAH

The Savannah gets its name from African grasslands where its close relative, the Serval cat, is to be found, which also helped lay the foundations for the breed, the first and subsequent generations having been derived from the breeding of a Serval with a domestic Bengal cat. The International Progressive Cat Breeders' Alliance (IPCBA) was the first all-breed registry to recognize Savannahs for inclusion. The goal of the Savannah breeding program was to create a domestic cat which had physical features linking it with the Serval, while at the same time imbuing it with the loving, dependable temperament of the typical domestic cat.

Appearance The Savannah has a large, muscular build, a long neck, large, round ears, and with distinctive black "tear-drop" markings on the eyes.

Characteristics and Temperament
It has a reasonably docile temperament, making it a great family pet that is easy to maintain. Savannahs are loyal, intelligent, and have an outgoing personality that makes them excellent companions for other household pets and children.

Coat The coat depends on the breed of cat used for the domestic cross. Early generations saw some form of dark spotting on a lighter coat, and many breeders used "wild"-looking spotted breeds, such as the Bengal and Egyptian Mau to preserve these markings in later generations. Coats colors include: Amber, Silver, Solid Black, Black Smoke.

"Thou art the Great Cat, the avenger of the Gods, and the judge of words, and the president of the sovereign chiefs, and the governor of the Holy Circle; thou art indeed...the Great Cat."
Inscription on a Royal Tomb at Thebes

SCOTTISH FOLD

In 1961 a Scottish shepherd noticed a cat with strangely folded ears. This cat, Susie, was the founder of the breed to which all of today's Scottish Folds are related. A breeding program was begun in the UK, but it was discovered that the dominant gene causing the folded ears was also likely to cause skeletal problems. The GCCF, among others, resisted recognition of the breed, and the main center of breeding activity switched to the USA. Today's Scottish Fold cats were developed originally by outcrossings to British Shorthairs and to American Shorthairs in the USA. They now resemble these cats in type, aside from the shape of their ears. Those with normal ears, often described as Scottish Straighters, are mated with cats which have folded ears in order to avoid genetic problems.

Appearance The Scottish Fold has a round face with wide, round eyes and with the ears folded tightly forward over the head. The ears should be small with rounded tips. The body is compact with a short neck. The tail is medium-to-long, flexible, and tapering to the tip.

Coat The short, soft, dense coat is kept in good condition with the minimum of brushing and combing. The ears should be gently cleaned inside the folds using a dampened cotton bud. There are both short- and long-coated versions of this breed, differing only in terms of the length of coat. Scottish Folds come in a variety of coat colors and patterns.

Characteristics and Temperament
A loving, placid, and companionable cat that is happy with humans as well as animals. They cope well with cold, harsh weather and have the farm cat's resistance to disease. Many Scottish Folds have the habit of sitting upright and tapping their owner with a paw. They often sleep on their backs with their legs in the air.

LEFT: The Scottish Fold's pixie-like look and placid temperament make them very popular pets.

SELKIRK REX

This naturally curly cat stemmed from a stray blue-cream and white non-pedigree kitten found in Wyoming in 1987. She was given to a breeder who mated her with a black Persian and she eventually produced three curly kittens out of six, proving that, unlike the Cornish and Devon Rexes (*pages 54–57*), the mother's mutated gene was dominant. Because of this, curly kittens can be born in the same litter as straight-haired ones. Several more breedings proved that she carried the genes for both point restriction and long hair. Because of this, the decision was made to allow all colors and both hair-lengths into the breed.

Appearance A medium-to-large cat with heavy bones that give it a surprising weightiness and an impression of power, which is a direct reflection of its Persian ancestry. The head is rounded with wide cheeks. The eyes are round, full, and widely-set. Ears are medium and pointed. The legs are medium and the paws large. The tail is thick and tapers to a slightly rounded tip.

Coat The cat has a random, unstructured coat, arranged in loose, individual curls that appear in "clumps" rather than as an overall wave. Maintaining the coat is the same as for a longhaired cat, while combing and brushing before bathing is necessary. All hairs are curled, including the whiskers.

Characteristics and Temperament

These are patient, loving, and tolerant cats with endearing personalities. Not many Selkirk Rexes are available as pets because most curly cats, especially females, are already involved in breeding programs. Both shorthaired and longhaired types are possible.

LEFT & BELOW: The Selkirk Rex is one of three breeds with a rex coat. The Cornish and Devon Rexes have short curly coats, while the Selkirk's is longer and wavy. It has a body which is similar to the Persian's.

SIAMESE

With their captivating looks, Siamese are among the world's most instantly recognizable breeds. They originated in Asia more than 500 years ago, where they were held in special regard as guardians of the Buddhist temples of Siam (now Thailand), and were looked upon as sacred by monks and royalty alike. In the late 1800s, the first breeding pair were brought to the UK. These were stockier cats with rounder heads than would become fashionable in later years. The popularity of the Siamese peaked around the 1950s, since when there has been a decline in their appeal, attributed by some to the move toward a more extremely elongated, angular look. Recently, however, there has been a resurgence of interest in a return to the more traditional "applehead" or classic look.

Appearance These tall and graceful cats have svelte builds, long, slim legs, and long heads. They are also fine-boned with taut muscles. Face-on, the head from the tip of the ears to the muzzle forms a pronounced wedge shape. The eyes are almond-shaped and slanted and a brilliant clear blue. The ears are prominent and pointed. The paws are dainty and oval, while the tail is very long, thin at the base and tapering to a fine point.

BELOW: Over the years, the Siamese has developed into an exotic looking breed. However, the original Siamese was a much stockier cat with a rounder head. This classic look is making a resurgence.

RIGHT: Siamese cats are vocal, sociable, and affectionate.

Coat The Siamese has a very short, fine coat that is glossy, silky, and close-lying. Grooming is easy but must be done regularly. Young cats are pale at birth and the coloration of their points only emerges gradually. Siamese cats come in a large variety of pointed coat-colors and patterns.

Characteristics and Temperament

An enterprising, lively and playful cat, the Siamese is loyal and affectionate but can be aloof at times. They are famous for their loud voices and big personalities and are better kept in pairs or small groups. Few cats are more ready to climb, both outdoors and in the home. Since Siamese cats become sexually mature early in life – sometimes at four months old, although six months is more usual – be prepared to arrange for young queens, in particular, to be neutered at the appropriate stage to avoid unwanted pregnancies.

SIBERIAN

According to legend, Siberian cats traditionally lived in Russian monasteries, where they protected granaries from rodents and patrolled the roof-beams on the lookout for intruders. In Soviet Russia cats were forbidden as pets and the Siberian did not develop a high profile until some of them arrived in East Germany in the 1980s, and a serious breeding program to standardize the type was begun. Imported into the USA since 1990, the Siberian, as a breed, is recognized by most cat organizations.

Appearance This large, sturdily-built cat has a broad head with a full, slightly rounded muzzle and a well-rounded chin. It has large oval eyes and medium-sized ears with rounded tips. The inner ear has an abundance of hair-tufts. The legs are thick and medium in length and the paws are large, round, and tufted. The tail is medium-length and thick, with a rounded tip. Recently, US bloodlines seem to be diverging somewhat from the traditional type, the body becoming more rounded rather than angular like that of a wildcat. Siberians are bred in a range of colors and varieties, with Tabbies, Tortoiseshells, and Bi-colors being relatively common, while Smokes and Self-colors may also occur.

Coat The topcoat is strong, plush and oily to ensure the cat's survival in the harshest conditions. The undercoat is dense enough to provide excellent protection against the elements, growing thicker in cold weather.

Characteristics and Temperament
A highly athletic animal, but at the same time sensible and resourceful. It is friendly while appearing to value its independence.

LEFT & RIGHT: The Siberian was originally known as the Siberian Forest Cat, the latter part of the name having been removed to avoid confusing it with the Norwegian Forest Cat.

SINGAPURA

During the 1970s an American cat-breeder found a colony of unusual-looking feral cats in Singapore. They were known as "drain cats," and at one time they were culled by the Singaporeans. The cats were first taken to the USA in 1975 and all registered Singapuras today originate from this breeding program. The name "Singapura" is Malaysian for Singapore.

Appearance Ranked as one of the smallest breeds in the world, typically weighing less than 6 pounds (2.7kg), the Singapura is nevertheless stocky and muscular in build. Its head is round, its ears large, and its eyes are huge, almond-shaped and colored a brilliant hazel, green, or yellow. The nose and eyes are accentuated as if dark eye-liner has been used. The tail is slightly shorter than the body and slender with a blunt tip.

Coat The fine, short, close-lying coat is in a ticked tabby with some markings on the backs of the legs but not on the front. Each hair should have at least two bands of dark ticking separated by light bands of color. Each individual hair is light next to the skin and dark at the tip. The Singapura is one of the few breeds that is only available – and accepted by cat registries – in one color. This is known as sepia agouti, being a warm ivory overlaid with sepia-brown, with paler underparts. Grooming is a simple matter, and a light combing is all that is needed to remove dead hairs, while occasional brushing will tone and stimulate the skin. Hand-grooming, or stroking with a silk scarf, will impart a healthy-looking sheen to the coat.

Characteristics and Temperament
The Singapura is affectionate, good-natured, extremely gentle, and playful. Unfortunately, it is still not widely available and ranks among the more costly breeds.

LEFT: The Singapura at first glance looks similar to an Abyssinian, but on closer inspection it looks quite different. Its coloring is more similar to a cougar's.

SNOWSHOE

The result of a cross between Siamese cats and American Shorthairs, the Snowshoe originated in the USA in the 1960s. The breed remained little known until the 1980s, since when it has gained in popularity but still remains quite rare. Snowshoes faced opposition from breeders of Siamese, who feared that its characteristic white feet-markings would become widely distributed in Siamese bloodlines if cross-breeding took place; but this proved to be groundless.

Appearance With the distinctive white feet that gave rise to its name, the Snowshoe retains the dark points of the Siamese on its legs, tail, face, and ears. Its eye-color is a bright, sparkling blue, while its muscular body is medium-to-large with medium-sized legs and a medium-to-long tail. The head is triangular, with large almond-shaped eyes that are slightly slanted, and it has large, pointed ears. As in the case of other large breeds, toms tend to be significantly heavier than queens.

Coat The short-to-medium, fine, glossy, close-lying coat needs only a minimum of gentle brushing. The cats come in the usual Siamese colors.

LEFT & RIGHT: The Snowshoe is a powerful-looking cat with great agility. It is known for its distinctive white feet that gave rise to its name.

SOMALI

The Somali is closely related to the Abyssinian, being its semi-longhaired version. Semi-longhaired kittens had occasionally appeared in the litters of the shorthaired Abyssinian over several decades. At first, these kittens were discarded and given away as pets, but it was eventually realized that a new breed was making a spontaneous appearance, the long fur being probably the result of a naturally long-established recessive gene within the breeding population. Somali to Somali pairings produce all Somali kittens, although their coats are shorter at this stage than those of adults.

Appearance The firm, muscular body is of medium build, with long legs and a long tail with a full brush of hair. The paws are oval and tufted, also the ears, which are large, cupped, and set widely apart. The head is a moderate wedge with a slight nose break in profile. The eyes are large and almond-shaped.

Coat The coat is soft, fine, and dense and lies flat along the spine. The coat-pattern of the Somali is quite distinctive, in that it is ticked, with three two-color bands on each hair. The coat is easy to groom, though the ruff and tail may need rather more attention. Somalis come in a variety of coat-colors including: Ruddy, Blue, Chocolate, Lilac, Sorrel, and fawn.

Characteristics and Temperament

Not quite as outgoing as the Abyssinian, the Somali is nevertheless unsuited to confinement to the house, and being a natural hunter thrives on vigorous activity. This is a charming, bright-eyed animal, with a cheeky air, which at the same time is gentle and receptive to quiet handling. It is soft-voiced, affectionate, and playful and is the perfect companion pet.

Typical Somali Varieties

Although different cat associations have their own rules for acceptance of new varieties, the Somali is recognized in most of the regular Abyssinian color varieties by most registration bodies.

RIGHT: The Somali has similar coat-patterns and coat-colors as its shorthaired counterpart the Abyssinian.

SPHYNX

The modern Sphynx breeding program began in 1966 in Toronto, Canada, when an ordinary shorthaired, black-and-white domestic cat gave birth to a hairless male kitten. The breed was developed from mother and son, and crosses with Devon Rexes were subsequently used to expand the breed's bloodline. The Sphynx is not popular with many cat fanciers, however, and is not widely recognized for show purposes because of health concerns resulting from the absence of a coat. This is a breed essentially suited to indoor living, away from the vagaries of wind and weather. The lack of fur makes these cats vulnerable to the cold, while exposure to hot sun can lead to sunburn, particularly over unpigmented areas of skin.

Appearance The Sphynx is a well-built, sturdy cat with a head slightly longer than it is wide, set on a long, slender neck. The large, wide-open ears are long, the outer edge being in line with the wedge of the face. Cheekbones are prominent and there are few or no whiskers. The cat has long, slim legs with elegant rounded paws and long toes. The tail is long and finely tapered. All colors and patterns are acceptable. Colors in the Sphynx are often warmer than they would be in cats with coats, because the natural pink of the skin is able to show through.

Coat The suede-like, wrinkled skin is covered with a soft, warm down, like the skin of a peach. There may be visible fur on the brow, around the toes, and at the tip of the tail. The skin needs daily cleaning, as the cat's empty hair follicles have oil-producing glands that cause it to sweat. Because it doesn't deposit hair on furniture or clothing it tends to be easier to keep homes clean, and it is therefore often less troublesome to mildly allergic owners. People normally

allergic to cats, therefore, may find that they can tolerate the furless Sphynx.

Characteristics and Temperament
A lively, playful, and mischievous cat, the Sphynx is very people-oriented, but does not like being held or petted. They are not too keen on other cats.

CAT FACT

The earliest ancestor of the modern cat lived about 25 million years ago. Scientists called it the Proailurus, which means "first cat" in Greek.

LEFT & RIGHT: The Sphynx is known for its extroverted behavior. It is very friendly and almost dog-like in the way it greets its owner at the door.

TEACUP

Origins It is said that Teacup cats originated in South America where they were found surviving in a back alley. They were caught and brought to Canada where they were bred successfully.

Due to their small size it seems that it is impractical to home them before 5 months old, otherwise they are normal healthy kittens. A good breeder will limit the number of litters to ensure that the queen stays healthy. Furthermore, this will help to safeguard the gene pool. Inbreeding should be avoided as offspring born from a diverse gene pool are more likely to experience good health.

Appearance Teacup cats are smaller than miniature cats that are usually about one-third to one-half the size of normal size cats of the same breed. As a guideline Teacup females weigh 2–4 pounds (0.9 kg–1.8 kg) while the males are 3–6 pounds (1.3 kg–2.7 kg). They are generally less than 9 inches tall when adult. Teacup kittens are more vulnerable than normal sized kittens. Being tiny can pose certain problems so they are relatively high maintenance.

Characteristics and Temperament A Teacup cat possess all the attributes of their larger cousins. They are popular with people who may live in a small house or apartment, or those who just like the idea of owning a small, kitten-like cat.

Coat Teacup cats are most commonly Persian in origin. They have long coats and come in the usual Persian colors.

LEFT & RIGHT: Teacups are basically little Persians, so require similar maintenance to their larger cousins.

TONKINESE

The Tonkinese displays the physical features of its
mixed parentage – the product of a mating between a
Siamese and a Burmese in the USA in the 1950s. The
Tonkinese has the points of the Siamese but with
softer body lines, having a less angular head and a
quieter nature. Breeding two Mink Tonkinese cats

does not usually yield a full litter of Mink-patterned
kittens, the Mink pattern being the result of having
one gene for the Burmese Solid pattern and one for

the Siamese Pointed pattern. The most likely result in such a mating will be one Solid kitten, one Pointed kitten, and two Mink kittens. All three coat-patterns will continue to exist and none can be bred out.

Appearance The Tonkinese is of medium build with a wedge-shaped head with high cheekbones and strong contours to the brow, cheek, and profile. The chin is firm and the eyes almond-shaped and slanted.

The ears have oval tips and the hair on them is very short. The legs are slim and the paws oval. The tail is medium-to-long and tapers.

Coat The coat is short, close-lying, fine, and soft, with a lustrous sheen. Very little grooming is required to keep the coat in good condition. Tonkinese come in a variety of colors and patterns.

Characteristics and Temperament

The Tonkinese has all the lively curiosity of an Oriental breed but without its loud insistency. It is a good choice for a person new to cats, being an easy cat to train, and it is also suitable for families with children. Tonkinese cats are fond of the outdoor life and should not be confined to small apartments or left to their own devices for hours on end.

LEFT: The Tonkinese, like the Siamese, is heavier than it appears due to its strong, muscular body. However, unlike the Siamese it is a quiet and placid cat — more like the Burmese in character.

TURKISH ANGORA

Angoras from Turkey first reached France in the 1500s. While the Turkish cat was an essential ingredient in the creation of today's Persian Longhair, its type was not as popular, and by the early 1900s, cross-breeding with other longhaired cats had led to its virtual extinction outside Turkey, while even in its homeland it was in short supply. A breeding program was organized in Turkey by Ankara Zoo; then, in the 1960s, the breed was imported into Sweden, the UK and the USA from Turkey. It has now been renamed the Turkish Angora to avoid confusion with the modern re-creation bred from Oriental stock in the UK, but early references in the 1900s to the Angora refer to this cat.

Appearance Graceful and athletic, the Turkish Angora is small to medium with a muscular body and an attractively tapered head. The eyes are large and almond-shaped. In the white variety, one eye is often blue and the other green. The ears are long and pointed, well-furred, and tufted. The paws are small, round, and dainty with tufts between the toes. The tail is long, tapering, and bushy.

Coat The medium-length coat is fine and silky with no undercoat. The fur is wavy on the belly. The cat is relatively easy to groom with daily brushing and combing. They molt heavily in spring, and can be mistaken for shorthaired cats during the warmer months of the year; but they can still be distinguished by the longer fur on their tails.

Angoras come in a variety of coat and eye colors.

Characteristics and Temperament
The Turkish Angora is a spirited animal with a sharp intelligence. It is often playful, while also appreciating periods of peace and quiet. It is a companionable cat with its owners but has a tendency to be aloof with strangers. It has a very loud voice and is an incessant talker. It can easily become destructive if left to its own devices for any length of time.

LEFT & RIGHT: Turkish Angoras have beautiful almond-shaped eyes. In the white variety the eyes are usually blue or amber or a combination of the two.

TURKISH VAN

In 1955, two cats were brought to the UK from their native Lake Van area of eastern Turkey. The breed spread across Europe, but acceptance by registries took some time, eventually achieved in 1969. In the US, TICA was the first to accept Turkish Vans for championship status, doing so in 1979, while the CFA followed in 1994.

Appearance A muscular cat with a long, sturdy body, the Turkish Van has a short, blunt, triangular head, a long, straight nose, and large, well-furred ears. The eyes are large, round and highly expressive. The legs are medium in length with neat, tufted, well-rounded paws. The tail is a medium-length full brush that perfectly balances the body. The coat is the most extraordinary feature of this cat, having evolved to cope with extremes of climate.

Coat The water-resistant single coat is thick in winter but very soft, like rabbit fur or cashmere, retaining the fine cashmere texture in summer. The coat is predominantly white, with auburn or cream markings on face and tail and a white blaze.

Characteristics and Temperament
Renowned as the "swimming cat" due to its habit of taking a dip in the waters of Lake Van, the Turkish Van will always swim if given the opportunity, and makes no objection to being bathed. It is an affectionate, self-possessed animal.

LEFT & RIGHT: The Turkish Van is predominately white with auburn or cream markings on the face and tail and body. Interestingly, the coat of the Turkish Van is water-resistant.

"He who rides the tiger can never dismount."
Chinese proverb

NON-PEDIGREE CATS

Of the 100 million or more pet cats worldwide, non-pedigrees (or random-breds or "moggies," if you prefer) vastly outnumber pedigree cats. Up until the end of the 1800s, cats were mostly kept in order to control rodents in people's houses and barns, and only the rich kept cats for their own sake. It was with the introduction of specific breeding programs that the concept of the pedigree (and therefore non-pedigree) cat was born. While some favor the looks, character traits, and habits of pedigree cats, a happy, healthy non-pedigree can be every bit as rewarding. Due to the endless possible combinations in their ancestry, their appearance and character is, of course, not completely

predictable, but a great many people feel it is a risk worth taking, for the sake of having a hardily dependable and friendly companion.

Appearance Some non-pedigree cats closely resemble particular breeds. However, most have the moderate build that is typical of the British and American Shorthairs. Apart from color and coat, non-pedigrees differ much less from one another than pure breeds do, having failed to acquire the extremes of cobbiness

LEFT & RIGHT: The non-pedigree cat is no less appealing than the pedigree. In fact, many people prefer them, in that they are usually more robust and live to a good age. They may not have the dramatic looks of some pedigrees, but all cats are beautiful in their own way.

THE CAT AND THE MOON

William Butler Yeats (1865-1939)

And the moon spun round like a top,
And the nearest kin of the moon,
The creeping cat, looked up.
Black Minnaloushe stared at the moon,
For, wander and wail as he would,
The pure cold light in the sky
Troubled his animal blood.
Minnaloushe runs in the grass
Lifting his delicate feet.
Do you dance, Minnaloushe, do you dance?
When two close kindred meet.
What better than call a dance?
Maybe the moon may learn,
Tired of that courtly fashion,
A new dance turn.
Minnaloushe creeps through the grass
From moonlit place to place,
The sacred moon overhead
Has taken a new phase.
Does Minnaloushe know that his pupils
Will pass from change to change,
And that from round to crescent,
From crescent to round they range?
Minnaloushe creeps through the grass
Alone, important and wise,
And lifts to the changing moon
His changing eyes.

LEFT: Apart from color and coat, random-bred cats differ much less from each other than pure breeds do. Most have the moderate build of the British and American Shorthairs, being neither slender like the Siamese or large and heavy like the Persian or Maine Coon.

or elongation that have been introduced into pedigree lines by selective breeding. Wedge-shaped heads and flattened faces are unusual in non-pedigrees but do sometimes appear if one of the parents includes a cat with Siamese or Persian genes in its recent history. Eyes are usually green or yellow, and most non-pedigree cats have fairly long noses.

BELOW & RIGHT: The random-bred cat has hybrid vigor, which is nature's way of ensuring the survival of the fittest. Non-pedigrees have much lower concentrations of undesirable genes, and with proper care should live to a ripe old age.

Coat Because the gene determining short hair is dominant, most random-bred cats are shorthaired.

Characteristics and Temperament

In general, non-pedigree cats are robust and energetic, having evolved over time so that only the fittest and most successful animals remain. A distinct advantage of owning a non-pedigree is that they have much lower concentrations of undesirable genes and are therefore less prone to disability and disease. With proper care, a non-pedigree cat should live a long life. The typical non-pedigree is a beautiful, intelligent, playful, low-maintenance companion, but with an independent streak.

Typical Colors Many non-pedigrees are tabbies, which is the variety closest to the cat's ancestor – the African wildcat – while Bi-Colors and Tortoiseshells are also common. Solid colors are less common, but black, white, marmalade (ginger), and blue do occur, usually broken with traces of white fur, typically under the chin. White is also common, both on its own and in combination with other Solid and Tabby patterns.

RIGHT: Many random-bred cats are tabbies. The Mackerel or Striped tabby pattern is the original, while the Classic blotched tabby is rather more common. Most rare is the Spotted tabby, now being selectively bred in new pedigree lines to achieve cats with a "wild" look.

CAT FACT

Non-pedigree cats with solid-color coats are less common than tabbies, but black, white, ginger (marmalade), and blue do occur, usually broken with traces of white, typically beneath the chin. Ginger coloring is sex-linked, carried in the X-chromosome, and ginger males outnumber females by about 2 to 1. Conversely, the Tortoiseshell or Calico pattern of orange-and-black is only possible in females, the rare exception being that it can also occur in sterile males.

LEFT: Some non-pedigrees have known ancestries; others may even have a pedigree parent or grandparent, but unfortunates are waifs and strays, rescued from one of the charitable organizations and with no known parentage. All deserve to be treated with the same love and care.

Chapter Four
CAT CARE
&
CAT BEHAVIOR

Bringing Your Cat Home

Once you have pondered the pleasures and pitfalls of owning a cat and decided to go ahead, it is vital to consider a thorough health check. The cat's coat should be silky and clean and free from parasites. The stomach should be soft with no lumps which could indicate the presence of roundworms. The ears should be clean and free from excessive discharge and parasites and the eyes, mouth, and nose appear healthy, while the anal area should be clean and unsoiled. Should any adverse signs be detected at this stage, it would be wise to withdraw from the transaction; the cat could have any one of a number of life-threatening diseases which could prove expensive to treat and traumatic for you should the cat die or have to be euthanized.

Before removing a cat from the care of its previous owner, it is wise to ask as many questions as possible relating to its health, likes, and dislikes. This makes life easier for you once you get the cat home, as rejected food and toys can be expensive mistakes. Make sure you also take away any vaccination records and pedigree certificates. In this way you can keep tabs on your cat's medical history and parentage. If any inoculations have lapsed or are due, get your vet to do them right away; this is not only life-threatening, it will also prevent you from boarding your cat if you suddenly have

LEFT & RIGHT: Whatever you choose, an adult cat or a kitten, first make sure that it is healthy. This handsome adult cat looks in the peak of condition and the kittens are lively and alert, always a sign of good health.

to be away from home. Proprietors of boarding facilities check very carefully that all inoculations are up to date; the last thing they want is diseases spreading to their other charges.

Choose the time of collection carefully as it is wise to be at home all day, every day, for the first few days to allow your cat to completely adjust to his new surroundings.

Make sure all necessary equipment and toys are purchased prior to arrival so that everything is on hand to allow the new arrival to settle in as quickly as possible.

Essential Items

Cat Carriers There are many different types of these available, constructed from plastic, wicker, or coated wire. They also vary in size, so make sure you select the correct one for your cat and remember that if it is young, it is likely to grow; allow for this fact when making your choice as it will be used throughout your cat's life for trips to the vet or boarding facility, or even when you move to another home, so it is best to choose one that is sturdily made, of good quality, and big enough.

Beds There are many types available and provided they are of adequate size and strength, most will be suitable. The traditional wicker bed and blanket or the beanbag are both popular choices. Beds with removable, washable cushions are particularly suitable, as regular washing helps prevent the spread of parasites and keeps them smelling fresh. To cut costs, most cats will be perfectly happy in a cardboard box with the front cut away. Old clothes or blankets can be added for warmth and comfort. Probably the most luxurious bed of all is the sheepskin hammock which fixes over the top of a radiator. During the winter, when the radiator is switched on, your cat will greatly appreciate this additional warmth and luxury.

LEFT & ABOVE: Make sure you have all your equipment on hand before bringing your new pet home. This way, the animal will settle into a routine with the minimum of fuss. This includes a carrier and a bed to sleep in.

Feed Bowls Purpose-made bowls come in many sizes but it is not strictly necessary to buy them; old kitchen rejects will do just as well. However, make sure animals' bowls are easily identifiable: it is not a good idea to mix them with utensils used by human beings for reasons of hygiene, and they should always be washed and dried separately. Cats' bowls should also be washed each time they are used. Make sure fresh water is available at all times.

Litter Trays Again, these come in a variety of shapes and sizes and some even have clip-on lids to prevent litter and bad smells from escaping. Depending on your budget, it is preferable to get the best you can afford as the smaller, flimsier trays allow litter to escape over the sides and the plastic is easily cracked. Buy a tray that is on the large side with reasonably

high sides which will take a good deep layer of litter; this is more economical in the long run. Soiled clumps should be regularly removed and the litter topped up, the whole lot being replaced at the end of each week. If you try to be too economical by using just a thin layer of litter, you will end up having to remove the whole lot every day.

If your cat is to be eventually allowed outside, the litter tray can be stored away and only brought into use at such times that you wish to restrict your cat to the home, e.g. when he is injured or sick.

For a cat which is to be kept permanently indoors, the litter tray will become a feature of its existence

BELOW: This wicker bed is partially enclosed, which keeps out drafts as well as offers a safe haven for a new arrival who may be nervous.

What to Look For in a Healthy Kitten

Nose Should be clean with no discharge or sneezing.

Mouth Breath should be pleasant-smelling, the teeth straight and white, and the gums pink.

Coat Should be clean and shiny, with no bald, itchy patches. Check for evidence of fleas.

Body Should be symmetrical and well grown. Body movements should be agile and supple.

Ears Should be clean and pink inside, free from discharge or redness and with no unpleasant odor.

Eyes Should be clear and bright, and the under-lids should be a healthy pink. There should be no redness or watering.

Anus Should be free from swelling or irritation as well as clean and dry.

Skin Should be clean and free from dandruff, blemishes and sore patches.

Limbs There should be no evidence of lameness. The kitten should be able to stand squarely and should be active and fluid in all his movements.

and it is best to find a convenient place for it away from areas where people gather for meals or tend to congregate. The scoop is a vital tool which will enable you to clean out the tray without getting your hands soiled. However, even if your hands do not touch the tray or litter, you should still wash them thoroughly afterwards.

There are many different kinds of litter, ranging from compressed pellets to fuller's earth and you will

LEFT: If you allow your cat is to go outside, make sure that it gets used to a collar from an early age, so that an address tag can be fitted in case it gets lost.

ABOVE: A cat flap is an ideal solution for cats who like to go outside, as they can come and go as they please.

soon find one which meets your cat's needs. Some prefer certain types and certain cats will reject litter which has a deodorant in it.

Grooming Tools It is a good idea to get your cat accustomed to being groomed from the very start. All cats need grooming, so purchase tools suitable for its coat length and type.

Collars A collar bearing a tag with your name and address on it is one of the best ways of identifying a lost cat or one which has been involved in an accident. The collar must be either quick-release or elasticated to allow it to come off easily should it become caught on a branch or other object.

Cat Flaps There are many types of these, but it is wise to choose a sturdy one as they take a good deal of punishment once your cat has become accustomed to coming and going. It is surprising how quickly cats learn to use them and once installed they will certainly make life easier for both cat and owner who no longer has to open and close doors each time the cat wishes to go in or out. In neighborhoods where there are many cats around, it can become a problem when next door's cat decides to come through your cat flap and into your home. If unwanted guests are a problem, you could choose a flap which can only be activated to open by a small magnet attached to your own cat's collar and will therefore not operate if other cats attempt to enter.

Toys Cats love to play and it is a good idea to get them accustomed to playing with their own toys. Small balls, string, or more elaborate manufactured toys can provide many hours of fun for both cat and owner.

Scratching Posts Cats need to try out their claws and mark out their territory and when allowed outside will use trees for the purpose. However, should he decide that the house is a place for scratching and that your sofa, stair carpet, or curtains are the targets or if he is an indoor cat with no access to a yard or garden, it is essential to get a scratching post.

ABOVE: To help protect furniture, provide a scratching post for your cat. There is a wide variety to choose from, ranging from a simple post covered in string to a more elaborate affair with a bed on top.

LEFT: Kittens love to play. There are plenty of purpose-made toys available that are safe for them to play with.

RIGHT: Offer your new arrival a warm and quiet place so it can settle in comfortably.

Settling In

The arrival of a new cat or kitten is an exciting time when you can at last spend time together, although a new environment will be enough to unnerve the most confident of characters. Make sure that you have transported your cat using some bedding taken from your own home which will accustom him to the unique smell of your house prior to his arrival.

At first, it is advisable to refrain from using vacuum cleaners, washing machines, and other noisy appliances so as not to alarm him. Once he is confident in his surroundings, you can begin to use them again.

Before releasing the cat from his carrier, ensure all doors and windows are closed to prevent a nervous cat from bolting and it is a good idea to restrict him to one room only at first. Once he has thoroughly settled, other rooms can be opened up to him which he can then explore at his leisure.

Allow your cat to wander out of his carrier, letting him sniff your hands before touching him and try not to make sudden movements. As his confidence grows it is important to reassure him by stroking him and talking to him gently and in a low voice. It may be his first experience away from his mother and it is therefore up to you to make him feel secure.

Shortly after his arrival, show him his food and water bowls, his litter tray and bed. Make sure you continue to feed the type of food he was accustomed to at his previous home. This way you will avoid possible stomach upsets during his first days with you.

It is important that his bed is warm and secluded and provided with plenty of bedding; at this stage, keep his water bowl, food, and litter tray close by.

From the very beginning, it is wise to establish certain rules, as cats seem to prefer a routine. If certain rooms in the house are to be out of bounds or you decide never to allow your cat onto your bed, establish this from the very start, keeping doors to forbidden areas firmly closed. If your cat has never been allowed to enter certain rooms, it is unlikely that he will persist in the future.

Should you decide to allow him to roam freely outside, it is important that you keep him restricted to your home for at least two weeks to allow him to establish his territory and gain confidence. It is a nerve-racking experience the first time you let him out and it is advisable that you accompany him and keep an eye on him the first few times he goes out alone. Cat or kitten, both must be fully vaccinated before being allowed out at all.

If the cat is to be perpetually confined to the house, make sure that he never gets a taste of freedom, or he will be forever trying to escape and may become listless and unhappy as a result.

BELOW: When your kitten is old enough, you may decide to let him go outside. Although there are dangers lurking, this is a more natural environment for him, and he will be happier as a result.

Handling Your Cat

The way you pick up a cat is most important, as doing this roughly or incorrectly could be injurious. Don't be tempted to pick him up by the scruff of his neck as a mother cat would her kitten. Pick him up by placing one hand under the chest just behind the front legs.

Next, place your other hand under the rump to support his weight, before lifting him up into the crook of your arm.

BELOW: When holding a cat, support its entire body. Never pick a cat up by its limbs or by the scruff of its neck as you could inflict a severe injury.

Meeting Other Pets

This can be tricky, but providing you are patient, things should work out well in the end. It is easier to introduce a kitten than an adult as a kitten poses less of a threat to an animal which is already in residence and immediately assumes a lower place in terms of the pecking order. As a kitten, it is more likely to accept a new situation and will often adopt passive postures, such as rolling onto its back to avoid a confrontation. The older resident animal will be understandably jealous of the new arrival, so expect a certain amount of hissing and spitting at first. Make sure you stroke both animals in turn, transferring their scents from one to the other. Cats have a good sense of smell and this will serve to bond them together. At this time, make sure you give an older, jealous cat slightly more attention. In this way he will be reassured that he is not being completely supplanted. Make sure you do not leave the animals alone together until you are completely satisfied that they have accepted one another and are now firm friends. The same procedure applies to introducing an adult cat, but be slightly more cautious that an aggressive situation does not develop which could eventually lead to a fight.

When a new cat meets the resident dog, special care should be taken as dogs can inflict great harm or death on a kitten and an adult cat could conversely injure a dog. Keeping the dog adequately restrained, allow the two to introduce themselves to one another gradually, repeating the process over a few days. Stroke both pets to transfer scents from one to the other. Allowing them to feed from their bowls while together in the same room will help consolidate the relationship. Whatever animal you are attempting to introduce to the other, do not leave them unattended until you are completely sure that it is absolutely safe to do so.

Cats and Children

Cats have always played an important part in family life and the birth of a new baby should not make parents feel that their cat is now redundant. However, there are sensible precautions you should take to ensure both baby and cat can coexist safely in the same house.

BELOW & OVERLEAF: Contrary to popular opinion, cats and dogs can get on very well together, particularly if both or one of them is a kitten or puppy.

RIGHT: Provided that you teach your children the correct way to handle cats and to respect animals in general, there is no reason why they should not become firm friends.

A cat will never intentionally harm a baby; however, they should not be left alone together. Babies in strollers or cots, surrounded by warm bedding, are liable to attract a passing cat who may decide to curl up for a nap on or near the baby's head. Therefore, make sure you use a stretch net cover, pulling it tightly over the cot to deter the curious cat.

In all households where pets live, and not only when a new baby is involved, hygiene should be paramount. Make sure you wash your hands after handling any animal and keep their toys and equipment well away from babies and young children.

Provided that a set of ground rules is observed, there is no reason why children and cats cannot mix successfully. From an early age, children must be taught the correct way of approaching and handling them and to treat them with the respect they deserve. It must be made quite clear that a cat is not a toy, but a living creature which should be treated as such.

Cat Safety

Keeping a cat safe from harm is the duty of every owner and, surrounded by so many dangers, we must do everything we can to minimize the risks to our pets.

In the case of a cat which is allowed outside, by far the greatest worry is that it may go missing and

BELOW: Cats have a canny way of finding hidden places to sleep. So if your cat goes missing, check the house thoroughly first.

we all tend to think the worst when such a situation arises. However, should your cat disappear for a longer period than is normal, be sure you make a methodical search before becoming too alarmed. You may believe he is still outside; however, it could be that he has returned home without your knowledge and has slipped into the closet for a nap or is curled up under a duvet. Make sure you look in such likely places before commencing your search in earnest. When checking outside, it is worth looking in sheds and garages and other outhouses to see if someone has inadvertently shut the cat away. Also check with neighbors in case the cat has slipped unnoticed through an open doorway or window and into their house. Finally, search the whole neighborhood, remembering to look up trees; cats love to explore high places and then become too afraid to jump down from them.

If, after a day, your cat has still not arrived home, you may wish to contact the police, animal rescue centers, and veterinary hospitals, who may have picked him up because he has strayed or has had an accident.

Tagging Have your cat tagged in order to set your mind at rest. Attach a metal tag which carries your name and address to an elasticated or quick-release collar, when anyone finding him can contact you immediately. Do not put your cat's name on the tag, as a thief could well use it to call him to entice him away. As a back-up to the collar tag, you may wish to consider an identity chip. A microchip is inserted into the loose skin at the back of the neck when it can be scanned and a number exclusive to your pet can then be read off on a display unit. All vets and animal rescue centers have the equipment to read these identichips and numbers are listed on a national data base, which will also hold the owners' details. It is also a good idea to add a tag to the cat's collar confirming that it is so equipped. The process of inserting the identichip is quick and painless and can be carried out at your local veterinary hospital.

ABOVE: In the USA it is not yet compulsory to microchip your cat or dog. However, it makes sense to do so, as a chipped animal is more likely to get reunited with its owner should it become lost or stolen.

The Danger Outside Most people feel at their happiest when they can see their cat happily perched on a fence or ledge in their own back garden. However, there are dangers lurking everywhere and responsible owners must be vigilant at all times. Cats are curious creatures and addicted to climbing, jumping onto window ledges, up trees, and onto roofs and they will happily scale walls and fences. Inevitably, they may overstretch their limits when they will be too frightened to climb down. Be ready to rescue your pet in a situation such as this, and keep a stepladder handy for the purpose.

It is commonly believed that cats do not like dogs and vice versa, and it is true that they sometimes prefer to steer clear of one another. However, there is always the time when an overconfident or unsuspecting cat will arrive face-to-face with a dog, perhaps in next door's garden. Nine times out of ten

Safety Outside

- Remove poisonous plants.

- Try to avoid living near busy traffic.

- Avoid ponds and cover swimming pools when not in use.

- Keep garden shed doors locked.

- Lock away garden fertilizers and weedkillers.

When choosing plants for your garden it is just as well to concentrate on ones which you know to be safe for animals. While it is rare for a cat to be poisoned by a plant, there are exceptions to every rule. Plants such as clematis, lupins, rhododendrons, and lily-of-the-valley are just some examples that should be avoided. Poisoning can also occur due to a cat consuming garden chemicals. It is preferable to avoid the use of slug pellets which are harmful to both pets and wild life, although there are special ones which reportedly do little harm. Other pesticides and herbicides can also be lethal to animals, so use them sparingly if you have to, and keep them in a shed or cupboard which can be locked.

Ponds and swimming pools are an obvious hazard, particularly to young or inexperienced cats. Should a cat fall into water, it is important that

the confrontation will result in the cat escaping over a fence or wall, leaving the dog to his own devices. Occasionally, however, a skirmish may result in one or both animals being hurt. If you suspect your cat has been injured by a dog, seek veterinary attention immediately as a bite may have caused some internal damage which is not immediately apparent.

Cats also occasionally fight among themselves, and injuries are unfortunately quite common, particularly in neighborhoods where there is a large cat population. Being territorial, cats like to regularly patrol their area to ward off other cats which are trying to encroach onto their patch. Neutered animals are less territorial and will be unlikely to get into a fight. It is therefore best to have your animal neutered if he is allowed to wander, as bites can become easily infected. If it is apparent that he has been fighting, check the coat carefully for deep bites which may need to be looked at by a vet.

ABOVE: Cat grass kits can be purchased from your local pet store. Your cat will love to nibble on the foliage.

there is an easy exit as it is very easy for a cat to drown. Fortunately, they do not like water and tend to avoid it.

You may prefer your cat to remain within the confines of your garden; this is a very tall order as cats are extremely good at climbing. It may be that you are worried about busy traffic in the vicinity, or even theft. A very high fence with the top sloping inward can be a deterrent, but it may be necessary to enclose the whole garden with a run constructed from wire netting.

BELOW & OVERLEAF: Cats are pretty clever when it comes to looking after themselves; even when they look as though they are in trouble, they invariably aren't. Cats love to climb trees and can usually climb down just as easily; sometimes, however, the young or inexperienced cat may panic and get stuck, and it will need your help.

Safety in the Home

- Keep all poisonous plants out of reach.

- Keep dangerous household products locked away.

- Unplug appliances not in use and remove dangling cables.

- Protect open fires with a fireguard.

- Keep cats and kittens away from upstairs windows.

- Keep cats out of the kitchen when cooking.

Keeping Cats Safe at Home

Even though we tend to worry more when our cat is outside, there are precautions to be taken to ensure that the inside of the house is safe. We already know how agile cats are and are frequently surprised by their ability to climb and jump to any height they choose. For this reason you have to make your house cat-proof at all levels.

Beware of open upstairs windows. Even though it is unlikely that a cat will try to jump out, it may inadvertently fall. Balconies are also lethal and if you live in a high-rise building you should forbid your cat the balcony unless it has been specially adapted to make it thoroughly safe.

The kitchen is particularly hazardous: do not allow your cat onto the worktops. This is not only

dangerous, it is also unhygienic. Knives, boiling kettles, hotplates, hot irons, and chemicals used in the kitchen are all potentially lethal. Beware of washing machines and tumble dryers. Check that they do not contain a sleeping or inquisitive cat before switching them on.

In the rest of the house, anything electrical is a potential danger and wires should be tidied away in order to prevent a playful cat from chewing through them. Any type of fire, whether open or otherwise, is a hazard. Remember that poisonous plants are not only encountered in the garden: many of our common houseplants, such as ivies, are poisonous and a bored cat may decide to attack a plant with unfortunate results. If in doubt, banish plants from your house altogether.

In the bathroom, make sure the lid of the lavatory bowl is always kept closed as cats are sometimes tempted to drink from them and could fall inside and drown or be poisoned by chemical cleaners. Never leave a bath filled with hot water unattended, not even for a minute.

ABOVE: Even though cats like high places, an open window such as this one can be lethal should the cat fall.

Feeding Your Cat

Cats are essentially carnivores, but a good diet should be a balanced combination of proteins, fats, minerals, vitamins, and water. It is essential that cats are fed meat, as they cannot survive on a vegetarian diet. In fact a cat's dietary requirements are quite complex and it is not necessarily a good idea to feed it entirely on fresh meat which may lead to a deficiency in certain proteins or trace elements. However, if this is your choice, you must feed an additional vitamin and mineral supplement. These supplements can be harmful if overfed, so check the instructions carefully. By far the best way of feeding your cat is to give it a combination of fresh and formulated foods. This will ensure a balanced diet and avoid boredom from having to eat the same food over and over again.

Pet food manufacturers make sure all the elements necessary for good health are contained within their products and instructions on the label will advise you on amounts to feed which are relevant to your animal's weight and age. There are many different formulated feeds available, ranging from those suitable for kittens and adolescents to special ones for older cats. Ultimately, careful feeding will be reflected in your cat's appearance. A well fed cat has a gleaming coat, bright eyes, and a lithe, well muscled body.

In their wild state, cats are hunters, catching and eating a variety of small animals. They usually consume the prey in its entirety, which includes muscles, bones, stomach contents, and even the head. Provided that you feed your cat the correct balance of food in small regular meals, you will be duplicating his natural feeding habits.

Water A vital component in sustaining all life, water is also necessary to ensure the correct functioning of the cat's digestive system, particularly when feeding it dried foods. Make sure clean, fresh water is available at all times.

LEFT: Cats and kittens require a well-balanced diet in order to stay happy and healthy. Feeding good quality formulated foods will ensure your cat gets all the nutrients he needs.

Rules of Feeding

- Feed little and often. At least 2–3 meals a day is best. Allow access to fresh water at all times.

- Serve food at room temperature.

- Watch your cat's weight. As a rule, cats do not suffer from obesity, but if you suspect he is putting on weight, ask your vet to provide a diet sheet.

- Only give special lactose-reduced milk formulated for cats.

- Kittens need special attention and must be fed more regularly than adults. Stick to specialist feeds and follow manufacturers' instructions carefully.

- Elderly cats need food that is more easily digestible, e.g. fish, rabbit, and chicken, complemented with formulated food.

- If your cat is ill, ask your vet what you should be feeding him.

- All small bones must always be removed from food.

- Do not feed foods which have been formulated for other animals, e.g. for dogs.

- Use clean bowls for each meal.

- Remove food which has been left uneaten and has become stale.

Milk Cow's milk can upset the digestion but if your cat loves milk, special lactose-reduced brands are available which will be easier for him to digest. Do not offer milk as a substitute to water.

Canned Foods Most cats are fed canned foods and there are many different brands and flavors from which to choose. As a general rule, try to feed the better quality ones which, though more expensive, will be more nutritious and contain less cereal to bulk them out. Follow the feeding instructions on the label.

Dried Foods Nearly all cats love dried foods which are less messy alternatives to canned foods; there is also less wastage as the food can be left out all day without it spoiling. They are complete foods, which means that you do not have to worry about keeping the diet balanced. The crunchy texture may help keep teeth in good condition. It is essential that when feeding dried foods, a clean supply of water is made freely available as little or no moisture is present in these types of foods.

Fresh Food Cats love to eat freshly cooked meat and fish and you could offer fresh food as a twice-weekly alternative to formulated foods, in which case you can be sure of a healthy balance. Make sure all food is properly cooked to avoid stomach upsets and take care to remove all small bones. The occasional can of tuna or sardines will also be a welcome treat.

Grass Anyone who knows cats will have noticed that they occasionally eat grass. It is thought that they do this to obtain folic acid and certain minerals, but cats usually vomit afterwards so it may be nature's way of cleaning out the system or of getting rid of fur balls. Cats which live permanently indoors can be given a tray of grass grown especially for them in a seedbox.

Cat Behavior

Cats are fascinating creatures, and even though they have adapted easily to a domesticated life, they still retain many of the traits of their wild ancestors and will readily revert to a feral state should the situation arise. Most of our domestic cats are well fed and watered but, even so, they still retain an atavistic instinct to hunt and continue to seek out prey, though now more for fun than necessity. For this, they remain well equipped with pointed teeth and razor-sharp claws; their eyesight is second to none and allows them to see in almost total darkness.

LEFT & ABOVE: Spraying and rubbing against objects are both ways that cats mark their territories.

Spraying This is the way a cat marks out its territory using its own urine. When a cat is urinating normally, it adopts a squatting position. However, when spraying, the cat's hindquarters are held high, and a jet of urine is directed at an object, usually a fence or a tree. All cats spray: it doesn't matter if they are male or female, neutered or unneutered, though unneutered animals are likely to spray more. This type of behavior enables cats to communicate with one another regarding territory, age, and sex and the

aim is to either attract or deter other cats to and from their territory. In general, spraying is only carried out outside; however, in certain situations, usually when the cat is under stress, spraying can occur indoors; however, this is short-lived once the source of the stress has been removed. A new pet added to the family, or a move to another house, are typical situations which may well be stressful to a cat.

Rubbing Against Objects Cats mark their territory in other ways and one of the most appealing is the way they rub themselves against us. Cats have glands in the head, body and tail that exude a strong odor which other cats can smell, but which is fortunately imperceptible to us. When cats mark their territory in this way, they are telling other cats that you are their property and are out of bounds. Cats do this everywhere, on you and your furniture, in the home and on fences, trees, and plants outside.

Scratching Cats love to sharpen and manicure their claws on trees and other objects that will allow them to get really stuck in. Some cats greatly prefer your furniture and carpets, which should be discouraged and a scratching post provided. Cats have scent glands on their paw pads so, as they scratch, they are also releasing an odor to mark their territory.

LEFT: Cats have two reasons for scratching. One is to keep the claws sharp, sometimes achieved by scratching your furniture and carpets, which should be discouraged. The other is another way of marking out territory, which the cat does by means of scent glands in its paw pads.

ABOVE: Nearly all cats have the potential to get into a fight, but you can reduce this possibility by having your own cat neutered. Cats also tend to fight at night, so keeping it in will help.

Fighting Because they are territorial animals, cats will often come into conflict with others of their species. Most prefer to avoid confrontation and neutering reduces the will to fight. Cats adopt various postures, depending upon whether they are showing aggression or submission. A puffed-up coat and tail will hopefully make an aggressor retreat and a cat which rolls over onto its back is indicating that it does not wish to fight. Fights between cats mainly take place at night, so avoid them happening by keeping your cat locked in. If you think he may have been involved in a fight, check him over carefully for injury.

Hunting Domestic cats do not hunt because they are hungry but because they enjoy stalking prey and their method is very similar to the way in which big cats and wildcats hunt. Using all their senses to track down their prey, they stalk silently through undergrowth, along branches, or crouch close to the ground. Once in range, in a split second they pounce to trap their victim. It is well known that domestic cats play with their prey rather than making a quick kill. This is possibly because they are driven to hunt by instinct and not hunger, in which case the kill would be quicker and more decisive.

Why Cats Purr It is not fully understood why cats purr, although it is generally thought to show contentment, even though cats have been known to purr when in pain. Purring is almost exclusive to felines, but hyenas make a similar sound when suckling. When we stroke a cat, purring usually

ABOVE: Cats which are well fed don't hunt because they are hungry but because they have an irresistible urge to stalk prey. This also explains why they cruelly play with their prey rather than going for a quick kill.

begins right away. There is no scientific explanation, but one theory is that the noise comes from the larynx, produced by muscles which close the vocal cords, which open when a rush of air passes through, causing this peculiar resonance.

The Senses

The cat has enhanced senses of sight, hearing and smell which make it a successful hunter. Cats can just as easily thrive in the wild, surviving on the small animals and birds they catch with remarkable skill and dexterity. Moreover, the acuity of their senses are

ABOVE: A cat's eyesight is highly developed and perfectly adapted to its role as a predator, particularly when hunting at night, when it can focus on the smallest of objects and pounce on them with remarkable accuracy.

combined with an astounding athleticism. These abilities have been passed down from the domestic cat's wild ancestors, along with a compelling urge to hunt.

Sight A cat's eyes are not only beautiful and striking but are also highly adapted to its life as a hunter. They are particularly effective at night; the pupil has the ability to dilate more fully than ours, allowing more light to hit the sensitive retina at the back of the eye. This enables the cat to see well when engaged in its nocturnal prowlings.

Hearing Cats can not only hear much better than human beings, they also perceive a wider range of sounds, including very high- and low-pitched noises imperceptible to us. Their ears can rotate though 180 degrees, enabling them to locate the source of the tiniest movement in the undergrowth. Due to their excellent hearing, it is not surprising that cats flee when the vacuum cleaner is switched on or we drop a saucepan in the kitchen – the sound must be deafening to them. It is this acute hearing, coupled with excellent night vision, which makes the cat a superb hunter, even of the smallest and fastest prey.

Smell A cat needs to sniff out its prey during hunting and its olfactory lobes are very well developed to perceive the faintest odor and also helps it to locate other cats. Cats have an additional attribute which some other mammals have and occurs when the upper lip is curled up to allow more scent to reach Jacobson's organ in the mouth. This is known as "flehming." This particular organ is not vital to the domestic cat's survival, but to his wild cousins it can be the difference between life and death.

Behavioral Problems

Much of what we consider "bad" behavior may be normal in a cat, but has become exaggerated due to certain circumstances such as stress. Spraying in the house is a case in point when a cat is feeling insecure and it is possible that he needs to mark his domiciliary territory to re-establish his confidence. Cats cannot be taught how to behave and they are not affected by punishment. The only way we can influence their behavior is through tact and immediate action. Try to look at the problem from

RIGHT: A cat's senses are extremely acute, particularly sight, hearing, and smell, all contributing to making it an excellent hunter. With a larger olfactory organ than human beings, the cat has a powerful sense of smell and can often be seen sniffing the air in the hope of detecting the presence of another cat or possible prey.

ABOVE: Cats are naturally clean animals and tend to cover their tracks after evacuating outside. Urinating indoors can be stress-related, maybe caused by the arrival of another pet or a new baby into the family. This should stop once everything has settled back to normal. However, make sure that your cat is not suffering from a bladder infection or kidney disease, as excessive urination may be a symptom of this; signs are listlessness.

your cat's point of view, which may make you more sympathetic to the situation. However, never rule out a medical disorder, which could be the root cause of the problem; veterinary advice should be sought in the first instance if you are at all worried. Confident, happy cats are less likely to become a problem, so it is important to socialize them from the time they are kittens when the incidence of unacceptable behavior will be kept to a minimum. Kittens should be allowed to interact with other animals, children, and adults. In this way, you can rule out situations which could alarm a cat once it is older and more set in its ways.

Spraying and Urinating Indoors It is important to know the difference between spraying and urinating. Spraying is the way in which territory is marked and usually occurs out-of-doors. However, once subjected

to stress, a cat may begin to feel threatened enough to cause it to mark its territory in the home. A new pet or baby in the house may well trigger this behavior and a change of circumstance such as moving house or the arrival of new carpet or furniture may also have this effect. However, spraying usually ceases once the cat has regained confidence. If he shows signs of insecurity, try to avoid situations which might upset him if at all possible. If this continues, consider having him neutered as this will possibly solve the problem. Your vet can also prescribe either hormone treatment or anti-anxiety drugs, which are also known to be efficacious.

Urinating indoors can also be stress-related. However, it is important that you make sure that your cat is not suffering from a bladder infection or certain other diseases. Check him out with your vet because cats are naturally clean animals and would not normally indulge in such behavior without cause. Make sure he has a fresh, clean, litter tray in a secluded part of the house as cats feel at their most vulnerable when evacuating. Also check that he is happy with the brand of litter in his tray and try changing it if not. Make sure you thoroughly clean all areas which have been soiled, as the slightest trace of a lingering odor may encourage him to re-offend. This applies to sprayers too.

Aggression Cats which have been overactive as youngsters often continue their boisterous behavior into adulthood, which is alarming for their owners who may suffer bites and scratches as a consequence.

ABOVE: Nervous grooming is a difficult behavior to cure. Tranquilizers may be prescribed as a last resort.

LEFT: Showing aggression should be discouraged.

A pouncing kitten is cute and harmless; however, this behavior must not be allowed to continue in adulthood. Cats which scratch and bite must be given plenty of toys to play with and if they persist must be scolded sharply whenever they re-offend.

Chewing Fabrics This is a strange habit, most common in the Oriental breeds such as Siamese and Burmese, which develop the habit of chewing and swallowing woolen clothing due to stress, leaving large holes in garments. This is an undesirable as well as an unhealthy habit, as wool can build up in the cat's intestine and require surgery to remove it. A solution to the problem is to remove materials which the cat finds attractive and to provide it with plenty of toys to play with as a distraction.

Nervous Grooming This can occur in any breed, but is most common in the Siamese. The cat becomes an obsessional groomer and doesn't seem to be able to stop licking itself, which causes sore, bleeding patches

ABOVE: Cats must not be allowed to eat house plants. The best option is to keep them out of the way of the cat.

RIGHT: Scratching at furniture and carpets is a big problem and you should discourage this type of behavior from an early age. Admonishing your cat with a stern NO every time he offends may help, but the instinct remains very strong.

to develop. This is very difficult to cure, although some owners have managed to break the habit by putting orange juice on the coat to discourage the cat from licking it. In severe cases, and as a last resort, tranquilizers may be prescribed.

Eating Houseplants Cats like eating grass in small amounts and in some instances may attack your houseplants as a grass substitute. This is usually a problem confined to cats which are kept indoors all the time, but all cats can develop the habit. If this becomes a problem, it should be discouraged, as many of the plants we keep inside are poisonous and dangerous if eaten. Even if the plant is not poisonous,

the foliage can be almost completely destroyed by a persistent animal; try to keep plants confined to a room which is out of bounds and do not ever leave your cat alone in a room with them. Try growing a tray of grass especially for your cat to chew.

Refusing Food One of the most alarming things an animal lover can imagine is the prospect of their pet refusing food and losing weight as a result. Cats are the worst offenders and while many seem to eat anything, others are so fussy that their food must be exactly of the right kind and at the correct temperature, otherwise they will simply not eat it. If this is the case, it is important that you try to discover your cat's preferences in order to keep it happy and healthy. Remember that cats like to eat little and often food that is fresh and at room temperature. The fussiest may refuse formulated foods and you may therefore have to feed freshly cooked food; there are very few cats which will refuse a piece of fresh fish or chicken. A diet consisting of fresh foods will require added supplements to make sure all the vital nutrients are present.

Scratching Furniture The tendency to scratch has the dual purpose of marking territory and sharpening claws. Most cats which are allowed outside have a

favorite tree or post which they use for the purpose, and cats that are never allowed out can be provided with a scratching post. However, this strong instinctual behavior can sometimes be transferred to the furnishings in your home and can quickly get out of control when carpets, sofas, and curtains are damaged beyond repair. If caught early enough, you may be able to deter your cat with a firm NO every time he offends, but he may persist when you are absent from the scene. A way of avoiding this happening is to exclude him from certain rooms when you are out of the house; another way is to choose soft furnishings which are unattractive to cats, e.g. leather or vinyl.

ABOVE: Cats have an overwhelming urge to stalk prey and birds seem to attract them most. Cats are contributing to the dwindling numbers of songbirds, much to the horror of their owners. Try to deter them as much as possible; fit your cat's collar with a bell which will warn birds of his approach and don't have a bird bath or feed the birds in your garden as you will be putting them in further danger.

Stalking Birds Cats are partly responsible for the decreasing number of songbirds, and owners are driven to despair by what they see as a cruel trait in their pets. Cats love to stalk any kind of prey, but it seems that birds attract them most, possibly because of the way they dart and flutter. Some cats actually eat their prey, while others bring them home as gifts to their horrified owners. If you consider that your cat's hunting habits have gone too far, you can frustrate him by attaching a bell to an elasticated collar to warn potential victims of his approach. This is really only a half measure as the problem seems impossible to cure completely, though it may diminish as the cat approaches old age.

The Timid or Nervous Cat It is difficult to restore confidence to nervous cats. Some cats which have been timid as kittens grow into timid adults, some do not, and it is not necessarily the case that cats that

have been cruelly treated when young grow up to be insecure. Whatever the case, you need patience, tact and understanding if you wish to improve matters. In extreme cases, symptoms of anxiety are panting, shedding fur, and crouching low to the ground, and

BELOW & RIGHT: Cats are timid or nervous for various reasons. They may have had an accident which has destroyed their confidence or have been previously ill-treated, or they may simply have been born that way. You can improve matters by being patient and understanding and by providing your cat with a quiet, calm environment to live in.

many cats simply bolt for a hiding place once they find themselves in a stressful situation. Provide your cat with a quiet place where he can get himself out of the way and sleep. When he ventures out, make sure you remain quiet and calm. Do not try to grab or pick him up, but allow him to come to you. Extend your hand and allow him to sniff it before giving him a gentle stroke and reassuring him calmly in a gentle tone of voice. Offer a few tidbits which will encourage him to come to you. In time, you may be able to instill more confidence into him and thereby increase his overall quality of life.

The Straying Cat A cat which has become accustomed to straying from home for long periods is a constant source of anguish to its owner, who seems to spend most of his time calling and scouring the neighborhood for his pet. Unneutered cats need a larger territory in which to roam and neutering may be a solution to the problem. Try feeding your cat at the same time each day. This way, you establish a routine and he will know to come home at mealtimes. Keeping him in at night will also help the situation and will save you from having a sleepless night worrying about him. In severe cases, also shut

him in for periods during the day, which may establish a more home-based lifestyle.

The ultimate way of controlling your cat's tendencies to roam is to fence your garden in such a way that he cannot escape. This can be done inexpensively with chicken wire or plastic-coated wire mesh. If you already have a high fence, extending its height is an easy matter, using wooden batons screwed together to make a frame construction

LEFT & BELOW: Most cats will wander off from time to time, but they are usually not too far away and will come to your call. Some, however, make a regular habit of disappearing for long periods of time. You may be able to curb this by establishing a routine, i.e. keeping him indoors at night and at certain times during the day. Alternatively, you may have to fence him in.

before fixing it to the fence. Tack the wire loosely in position to cover the frame, using small fencing staples and allowing about a foot to overhang along the top; this will deter most cats from jumping over. Check at ground level along the boundary, blocking up any gaps as you go.

The alternative to this is to construct a cat run using similar materials. Ideally, the run should be connected to the house, enabling the cat to come and go as he pleases through a cat flap. The advantage of this arrangement is that you can also keep his litter tray, feeding bowls, and other equipment outside, which will keep your house cleaner and odor-free. If the cat run is positioned a distance away from the house, be careful when transporting him to it in case he escapes. If you think this possible, always use a cat carrier.

On the Move

At some time or other in your cat's life he will have to travel, at least once a year to the vet for his annual booster and, if you like to take a vacation, to a boarding facility.

Traveling Generally speaking, cats are not good travelers, though you will find that those which have traveled regularly from an early age adapt better to the unnatural movements of vehicles and aircraft. For most journeys you will need a well constructed cat carrier containing plenty of comfortable bedding. If the journey is likely to be a long one, you will also need to line it with newspaper in case the cat vomits or has diarrhea. Make sure you take plenty of cleaning materials in case they are needed to clear up after an accident and provide plenty of clean, fresh water. If your cat is prone to vomiting, do not feed him immediately prior to a journey, but make sure you give him a small meal earlier in the day. In the case of a very nervous traveler, it may be necessary

BELOW: As rule, cats don't like traveling at all. However, providing them with a sturdy carrier filled with comfortable bedding will go a long way to ease the situation and prevent them from becoming too alarmed.

to consult your vet who may prescribe sedatives. However, do not administer any drug without veterinary advice.

Do not be tempted to allow your cat out of his carrier in the course of a journey, as once out he may panic, causing possible distraction to the driver of the vehicle. In hot weather, take extra precautions

BELOW: Always secure your cat in a sturdy carrier placed on a flat surface and tied firmly down in case of accident. Never let a cat run loose inside a car; even if a person is holding him, he could still break free and cause considerable havoc.

that the animal does not become overheated. Make sure there is adequate ventilation and under no circumstances leave your cat unattended in a car.

Some cats begin to associate being put in a carrier with unpleasant experiences, such as visiting the vet or traveling in the car, so that whenever the carrier is produced he may try to flee. In such a case, it is a wise precaution to close cat flaps, doors, and windows first and restrict the cat to one room in the house before placing him in the carrier. When doing this, make sure you hold him gently but firmly, as he may attempt to wriggle out of your grasp. Make sure you close the carrier door as quickly as possible without causing alarm and double check that the

catch is fastened to prevent the cat from escaping in a strange place, resulting in a lost and very frightened animal.

When taking your cat abroad, not only should you ensure that he will be comfortable on the journey, but you should also check out border restrictions and any other problems which may occur. Many countries and states restrict entry to avoid the spread of disease. If entry is permitted, it is likely that proof of vaccination as well as identity will be needed. In all cases, make sure you familiarize yourself with all requirements some months prior to departure. If you are traveling by air, contact the airline beforehand, which will advise you on equipment and other documentation you may require. In Britain, for example, inoculation against rabies was once only used on animals intended for

export but now that quarantine regulations have been changed it is mandatory.

Moving House Moving to a new house is a traumatic experience and it is easy to forget your cat's special needs at this difficult time. Cats do not relish changes of environment or their routine disturbed, so it is up to you to make the process go as smoothly as possible.

For a few days leading up to the event, allow your cat to become accustomed to one particular, quiet room in your house. Lock him in that room for a few hours each day when he will become accustomed

BELOW: When moving house it is advisable to keep your cat indoors for at least two weeks so that he can become used to his new surroundings and less likely to run off in panic.

to the routine. On the day of the move, lock him away in his room before the chaos commences and ensure that all family members and the removal team know that they must not enter until last thing – put a notice on the door to discourage entry. Once the whole house has been cleared, carefully transfer your cat to his carrier, taking his bed, water, and feed bowls and any other paraphernalia, and transport him to the new house in a manner likely to create the least disturbance. Once there, set him up in a similar quiet room accompanied by his toys, bed, and familiar objects from the former house. Make sure all windows are closed to avoid him bolting and ensure that no one is likely to open the door.

Once the process of removal is complete and all the furniture is in place and the removal team have departed, you can begin to allow your cat restricted access to other rooms in the house. If you permit him to explore just a few rooms at a time, you will avoid confusing and alarming him. Most cats will have calmed down within a few days and will soon assume the run of the entire house. However, at this early stage, it is vital that you do not allow him outside, as being unfamiliar with his new surroundings he may run away and not know how to return. Confine him to the house for at least two weeks before letting him outside, by which time you can be sure that the cat now knows where he lives.

When you first let him outside, make sure you keep an eye on him or even accompany him into the garden, as this will reassure him. At first, let him

BELOW: After two weeks, allow your cat to explore a little further under your supervision.

outside before he has been fed, which will get him into the habit of returning home for meals. Eventually, he will carve out his new territory and make new acquaintances; fortunately, cats adapt relatively quickly to new surroundings.

There are some who may wish to avoid putting their cat through the whole trauma of moving by taking it to a boarding facility before packing up, and introducing it to the new house once the process has been completed.

Boarding Most cats, at some stage or another during their lives, need to be boarded, and vets or friends will often be able to make recommendations. However, it is still wise to visit the establishment personally prior to making a booking to check out its suitability. Reputable facilities are likely to welcome an inspection and will provide a guided tour. During inspection, make sure you ask to see the price list, ascertaining

any hidden extras or insurances which may be necessary. If you intend to travel during the peak holiday period, book your cat in well in advance, or as soon as your trip is confirmed. Boarding facilities can quickly fill up in the summer months and it can be very worrying and disappointing when you discover that the better ones are already fully booked.

The boarding facility should be immaculately clean, well maintained, and of sturdy construction. All the runs, beds, and equipment should have been disinfected between use to avoid the spread of infection, and for the same reason cats should be kept apart. Bedding material should be disposable. Furthermore, it must be secure enough to ensure no cat can escape and the enclosed area should have at

BELOW: Following a move, your cat will soon have completely forgotten his old home and will have settled down happily in his new one.

least two sets of doors to be doubly sure. In winter, heating should be provided in the sleeping areas.

Proprietors of reputable establishments will always check that a cat's vaccination record is up to date before accepting it; so never allow vaccinations to lapse. On arrival, you will be asked to fill out a registration form and also a list of your pet's likes and dislikes as well as any food preferences he may have. You will be asked to provide an emergency contact number for the period that you are away. You may also be asked to provide your own vet's name and address.

It may be permissible to leave your cat some of his favorite toys to reassure him while you are away. The first time you leave him at a boarding facility, he may initially appear distressed as you walk away. However, he will soon acclimatize to his new surroundings and in a short time will settle down. If you have two cats, they can be housed together in a shared pen which will ensure that both cats settle down very quickly.

When collecting your cat after a trip away, check him over for general health and examine him for parasites in particular, such as fleas. Even vaccinated cats can pick up minor colds and infections and if you think this may be the case, consult your vet immediately. Remember to ask the proprietor how your cat has fared, as you may wish to use the establishment again.

In rare cases, cats may fret to an unacceptable extent when you may have to obtain the services of a house-sitter while you are absent from home.

BELOW: When the time comes for your cat to spend time at a boarding facility, do plenty of research to find out the best establishment in your area.

Grooming

Cats are fastidious creatures and naturally spend a good deal of their time grooming themselves. Because of this, there is a misconception that this is all they require. However, all cats benefit from a daily grooming session and provided that this has been done from an early age, will actually grow to enjoy the process. Grooming helps clean the coat and reveals evidence of parasites. It is also a good opportunity to check a cat's general state of health; anything you notice which worries you should be reported immediately to your vet.

Claws As well as giving the body a thorough grooming, there are also other areas which require special attention. Cats which venture outside do not usually need their claws clipped, but some cats, particularly those confined to the house or elderly ones, may require regular attention. Also check cats which go outside for injuries. Make sure you use clippers which have been specially designed for the

purpose. Only a small area of the claw should be removed, taking care not to cut into any sensitive parts. Ask your vet to guide you through the process before trying it yourself.

Eyes Cats' eyes are invariably clear and bright, but sometimes they do require attention. Always take the greatest of care when cleaning around the eyes and use a piece of cotton wool dampened with a preparation designed for the purpose or water. Do not touch the eyeball directly and make sure no fibers enter the eyes.

Ears Before cleaning, inspect the ears for disease. If there is a dark discharge, consult your vet. Clean the ears in the same way as the eyes and never use cotton buds or other implements.

RIGHT: Shorthaired cats only require a quick brush over a few times a week, as the coat is not prone to matting. However, this regular grooming helps keep the skin and coat healthy and gleaming.

Teeth Older cats tend to suffer from gum problems which can be caused by a build-up of tartar on the teeth. It is therefore a good idea to accustom your cat to having his teeth cleaned from an early age. It is not necessary to do this every day, weekly will suffice. Use a small soft toothbrush and a specially formulated toothpaste for cats to gently clean the teeth. If this causes distress, try a cotton bud and toothpaste which is less disturbing.

Grooming the Coat Whatever coat type your cat has, whether short, long, fluffy or double-layered, there is a comb for the purpose. Longhaired cats require rather more attention and will need a daily grooming session. For shorthaired varieties, grooming is not so vital, although many owners groom daily because their cats enjoy it so much.

First use a soft brush and once the knots are removed the coat can be combed through. Discourage the cat from turning the process into a game. If the coat has become matted and you feel you cannot remove the mats through ordinary grooming, you may need to have them removed by your veterinary surgeon. Don't allow the coat to get into this state in the first place.

LEFT: Grooming, particularly for longhaired cats, should be a daily routine. Not only will it prevent painful knots from forming, it also presents an opportunity to check your cat over for uninvited visitors such as fleas and ticks.

Grooming Health Check

- Check that the skin is clean and pink, with no dandruff, lumps, or abrasions.

- Check for evidence of fleas, looking out for feces.

- Check that the eyes are clean and bright with no redness or discharge.

- Check that the ears are clean and odorless with no discharge.

- Check that the teeth are clean and white with healthy pink gums.

- Check that the claws aren't overgrown.

- Check that the anus is clean, dry, and free from swellings.

Health Matters

Keeping your cat in peak condition should be your primary concern, as an unfit cat is an unhappy cat. Moreover, some disorders which affect cats can threaten other animals as well as people in the household. Provided your cat appears to be in good health, he will need a yearly checkup by a vet, which is a convenient time for his vaccination boosters to be given; following this, it is up to you to monitor his health. A healthy cat has an alert expression, bright eyes, a clean nose, ears, and rear, a shiny coat and a lithe body. His disposition will be happy and playful and he will find it easy to relax and sleep comfortably. A good appetite is also a sign of good health. If you think there may be something wrong, look at the skin and coat. Check the ears, eyes, nose, and mouth. A runny nose may be a symptom of a cold or a weepy eye could indicate an infection. If you are in any doubt, seek veterinary assistance.

Common Problems

Fleas The flea is a common parasite, causing skin problems which result in constant scratching and washing which is distressful and which will impair the cat's overall condition. Usually fleas do not cause serious health problems; however, a severe allergic reaction can sometimes be triggered by their presence. Whatever the case, fleas do need controlling and must not be ignored; remember that warm weather increases flea numbers. If you suspect that your cat has fleas, pass a fine-toothed comb through his coat, particularly around the neck area, tapping it onto a piece of white paper. You will know you have a problem when tiny blackish flecks appear on the paper. These are flea droppings.

These days there are many different ways of controlling these pests which include injections and drugs. However, the most usual method is still an insecticide spray which should be recommended by your vet and obtained from his surgery. Always follow the directions carefully, as some sprays are harmful if breathed in or allowed to come into contact with human skin. Flea collars are a useful control method and provide a continuous flow of insecticide. Make sure the collar is elasticated and watch out for irritation as an allergic reaction can sometimes occur.

If fleas are present on your cat, they will also be in your house. Your vet will advise you on the types of sprays suitable for household use. Do not use these on your animals. Vacuuming carpets and soft furnishings regularly, while paying particular attention to all the nooks and crannies, and especially carpet edges, will help reduce the number of flea eggs in the home, serving to break the cycle of infestation.

Controlling the incidence of tapeworms will also greatly help the situation.

The presence of animals in the household calls for even greater hygiene. Get into the habit of keeping your house and your pets' sleeping areas spotlessly clean. This will reduce the likelihood of parasites such as fleas becoming a problem in the first place.

Kittens infested with fleas are a special case, so consult your vet who will prescribe the correct form of treatment. On no account apply a flea spray to a

BELOW: Excessive scratching can be a sign that your cat is suffering from a skin disorder or a flea infestation – not a serious problem if treated promptly.

kitten under 7 weeks old. Instead, use a fine-toothed comb to remove the fleas and keep the bedding area scrupulously clean.

Ticks These are mainly a problem in rural areas where there is long grass, although they can be picked up anywhere. Ticks attach themselves by their mouth parts to the cat's head and neck area, feeding on the animal's blood for 4–5 days before dropping off. In some cases, a heavy infestation can cause anemia. A bloated tick is gray-blue in color and is the size of an apple pip. As spreaders of disease, it is important to rid the cat of ticks as soon as they are noticed. Do not attempt to pull them off – the mouth parts may

remain in the cat causing infection. Instead, use a flea spray and after about 24 hours the dead tick can be removed using tweezers. Make sure the tick comes away from the skin intact and destroy it by burning.

BELOW: Being vigilant and noticing when things are not quite right will go a long way to keep your cat healthy and happy. Make sure that the eyes are bright, the nose and ears are clean, and that the coat has a healthy sheen. Worm regularly and make sure that he is fully vaccinated and has his yearly booster.

Mange Fortunately, mange is a rare complaint in most countries. It is caused by a microscopic parasite called *notoedres cati*, which burrows under the cat's skin causing intense irritation. If you suspect your cat to be so afflicted, isolate him immediately and contact your vet.

Ear Mites These spread easily and are common in cats and kittens; your vet can prescribe ear drops to cure the complaint. The tiny mites cause irritation of the

ABOVE: Yearly booster vaccinations are vital, and your vet will also give your cat a general health check.

skin, resulting in head-shaking and the secretion of a dark-brown ear wax which is clearly visible inside the ear.

Fur Mites At first glance this appears to be dandruff spreading along the animal's back, but is in fact an infestation. Fortunately, it is a rare condition. Treat with a flea spray.

Harvest Mites These appear as tiny red dots and are usually found around the ears and between the toes. Treat with flea spray.

Ringworm This is a highly contagious fungal condition which can spread throughout many species of animals as well as human beings. The disease is characterized by scaly patches on the animal's skin. In humans, the condition is more easily recognized and takes the form of red circular patches. If you suspect ringworm, consult your vet immediately who will advise and prescribe treatment. The disease can also be spread through bedding, feeding bowls, or almost anything with which the animal comes into contact; everything must be burned once the infection has passed. When treating, wear gloves and thoroughly wash your hands afterwards. Treatment can take many weeks, which means that the animal must remain in isolation until completely cured.

Internal Parasites

Worms For cats which venture outside, and in particular those which hunt and eat their prey, worm infestations are not uncommon and most cats will be

Signs of Illness

The more you get to know your cat the easier it is to sense when he is unwell. He may not be as lively as usual or he may hide himself away when he is usually under your feet. Watch closely, and you will notice if he presents any of the following symptoms:

- Excessive vomiting.
- Loss of appetite.
- Pain in the mouth.
- Weight loss, both sudden or prolonged, weight gain.
- Fever/lassitude, labored breathing.
- Excessive thirst.
- Prolonged diarrhea.
- Coughing.
- Choking.
- Sneezing.
- Frothing at the mouth.
- Increased urination/inability to urinate.
- Itching, scratching, and head-shaking.
- Lameness.
- Fits.
- Eye, ear, or nose discharge.

afflicted from time to time. Worms live inside the animal, feeding on digested food. Your vet can prescribe a regular worming program to ensure that your cat is protected. Different species of worm are affected by different drugs making it essential that you seek veterinary advice.

Roundworms Kittens are most likely to pick up roundworms, which are contracted through their mother's milk. Diarrhea or constipation, weight-loss and general deterioration in condition are all symptoms and the kitten may also have a pot-bellied appearance. If they are passed in the animal's stool the worms resemble lengths of white thread. As it is a riskier situation for a tiny kitten to be ill, your vet should be consulted as soon as symptoms are recognized. In fact, all kittens should be wormed regularly from the age of 6 weeks and pregnant cats should also receive treatment. Your vet will prescribe a suitable worming program.

Tapeworms These attach themselves to the wall of the host's gut and can grow very long. They are made up of egg-filled segments that separate off and are passed with the cat's motions. The first sign of infestation is when you discover a small, white, moving object attached to the cat's rear end. This is a segment which has broken away from the rest of the worm in the cat's gut. All cats should be wormed every 6 months and you will need special advice from your vet when worming kittens. It is important that your cat is regularly treated for fleas as they can cause re-infection. The tapeworm larvae develop within the flea which, if ingested by the cat when licking its fur, will cause a further infestation.

Toxoplasmosis *Toxoplasmas gondii* are microscopic intestinal parasites which use the cat as its primary host. They usually live in the bowel and shed their eggs which are passed in the cat's motions. An infected cat rarely shows symptoms but the disease is transmissible to humans and is very dangerous as it can cause damage to unborn children. It is most important that pregnant women do not touch cats'

RIGHT: As you get to know your cat you will almost instinctively know if anything is wrong. With yearly health checks from your vet, good nutrition and care, you will be able to prevent many common illnesses from occurring.

litter trays and the job of changing the litter is best left to others. However, whatever the circumstances, hygiene is of prime importance when cleaning up after any animal. Litter trays should be regularly disinfected and hands thoroughly washed. To keep matters in proportion, though, infection is rarely passed to human beings by pets, being more likely to occur through handling uncooked meats or dirty vegetables.

Other Conditions

Fur Balls When cats lick their fur to clean it, there is always a certain amount that is ingested. Some cats, particularly those with long fur, can swallow quite a lot and the loose hairs cause a matted ball within the stomach. Once the ball grows to a certain size, the cat will vomit it up. If your cat is prone to this condition, make sure he is groomed regularly, removing most of

LEFT: Fur balls are particularly common in longhaired cats, but the problem can be considerably alleviated by daily grooming, which will remove most of the loose hairs.

ABOVE: Eye problems should always be treated by a vet.

the loose hair before he has time to swallow it. If you are worried about the condition, consult your vet who will advise special treatment. A simple remedy you can use at home is to dose your cat with a fish oil or a small amount of olive oil to lubricate and soften the fur ball, which will more easily pass through the system.

Eye Conditions

Conjunctivitis Fortunately, this is a rare disease in cats and is usually caused by a scratch or a foreign body entering the eye. The infection causes the eye to become inflamed and if left untreated can become ulcerated. Consult your vet immediately.

Eye Injuries Most injuries to the eye area occur when cats fight. Provided that the wound is small and not actually in the eye, it will usually heal without problem. However, if the wound is deep or close to or in the eye itself, it could be more serious and your vet should be consulted without delay.

Watery Eyes Some cats, particularly pedigree types, are susceptible to this condition which is usually caused by an overactive tear duct. However, if you suspect the watering is being caused by an irritation, a blocked tear duct, or another disease, or if the discharge is offensive, consult your vet immediately.

Ear Conditions

Ear Infections The ear canal can become inflamed due to a fungus or bacteria or in some cases the introduction of a foreign body. If your cat continually scratches his ears or there is a discharge coming from them, consult your vet who will usually prescribe ear drops.

Hematoma A hematoma, or blood-filled blister, can develop on the cat's ear and is usually the result of having being scratched while fighting. As the ears are very sensitive, hematomas can be painful and will need draining as they will not disappear of their own accord. This should be carried out by your veterinary surgeon as soon as you notice the condition.

Mouth Conditions

Wild cats have a varied diet and much of the food they eat involves a good deal of chewing and gnawing, which cleans the teeth, strengthening them in the process. Many of the processed foods we feed today do not act as positively on the teeth and therefore it is not surprising that many of our domestic cats have gum and tooth problems.

All cats can suffer from dental problems. However, it is the older ones which are most susceptible and a build-up of plaque or tartar on the surface of the teeth can lead to infection and inflammation of the gums (gingivitis). Bad breath or

ABOVE: Deposits of a light brown substance called tartar can build up on the teeth, leading to gum irritation and gingivitis.

problems with eating are signs that all is not well. Check your cat's teeth and gums regularly and accustom him to having his teeth cleaned weekly. Consult your vet if you are at all concerned.

Gingivitis This is an infection of the gums, the first sign of which is a red line of inflammation between tooth and gum. The condition is extremely painful and will require veterinary attention. Clean your cat's teeth and gums regularly. A lightly cooked chop bone is ideal for him to gnaw on and will help remove debris from the teeth and strengthen the gums.

Respiratory Problems

At some point in their lives, nearly all cats present cold-like symptoms. Sneezing, coughing and labored breathing are common signs, but also watch for runny eyes and noses. Usually the condition is mild and disappears after a day or so. Should the symptoms persist or worsen drastically, however, veterinary attention should be sought immediately.

Feline Respiratory Disease (Cat Flu) There are two respiratory diseases commonly known as cat flu, one being Feline Calici Virus (FCV) and the other Feline Viral Rhinotracheitis (FVR). The symptoms are fever, coughing and sneezing, runny eyes and nose. The condition may cause the cat to temporarily lose his appetite due to a reduction in his sense of smell. FCV can cause painful mouth ulcers, but it is FVR which is the most dangerous of the two types. The disease affects the nose, trachea, and lungs and breathing can become very difficult. Kittens and older cats are particularly at risk as they may not have the stamina to recover. In any case of flu, attention should be sought as your vet may wish to prescribe antibiotics to limit the spread of a secondary bacterial infection. Flu patients require careful nursing and feeding as well as plenty of rest, and gentle bathing of the eyes and nose will make the cat feel more comfortable. Unfortunately, the virus can persist in the cat's system after recovery and should it later fall ill or be under stress, the virus can be shed, infecting other cats.

As always, prevention is better than cure, so make sure your cat is vaccinated; all cats should be vaccinated as kittens at 9 to 12 weeks with a second vaccination one month later, and given regular boosters annually.

Chlamydial Disease This is a disease of the respiratory system and produces flu-like symptoms. The condition is quite rare, but more common where large numbers of cats are congregated together, as in breeding establishments. Even though the risk is small, the disease is transmissible to human beings, so hygiene must be strictly observed when symptoms are present. Always wash your hands after handling an infected or suspected case. It is possible to vaccinate against the disease, so if you think your cat or cats are at risk, consult your vet.

Digestive Disorders

Feline Infectious Enteritis (FIE) This is a serious viral disease which is highly contagious and an infected cat is unlikely to recover. The virus affects the digestive tract and persistent vomiting, fever, bloody diarrhea, depression, and severe dehydration are the symptoms. Infected cats must be isolated at once and will require immediate veterinary care when intravenous fluids will possibly be introduced. Treatment is rarely successful and in order to prevent further infection, your whole house will need to be decontaminated. Your vet will be able to advise you on this. If you intend to introduce a new cat into the environment, make sure it has been vaccinated for FIE at least two weeks previously. Vaccinations, with yearly boosters, are essential to prevent cats from contracting this terrible disease.

Feline Infectious Peritonitis (FIP) This can strike cats of any age, although younger ones are more susceptible and have less resistance. The virus which causes the disease is called Coronavirus (FCoV). Many cats throw off the infection with few signs of the disease, but sadly some cats go on to develop the full-blown version which is fatal. The virus affects the abdominal cavity, liver, kidneys, brain, and nervous system. There is no cure and no vaccine for this disease and therefore patients must be isolated before death to prevent infection from spreading. Fortunately, the virus is not very resilient and is easily destroyed through disinfection; it can only survive at room temperature for a couple of days.

Diarrhea This has many causes, including a change in diet and a stressful situation. Mild diarrhea will pass very quickly; however, if it persists longer than 24 hours, or is accompanied by vomiting or blood is present in the stools, it could be a sign of a more serious disorder, so consult your vet immediately. During any case of diarrhea, the most common complication is dehydration, so it is important to make sure fresh water is freely available at all times.

Constipation This is a common condition, but is more likely to afflict elderly cats. If you notice your cat straining to produce a motion, try to establish that it is a stool that he is trying to pass and not urine. A cat unable to pass urine should be treated as an emergency and immediate veterinary attention is essential. In mild cases you can treat constipation by feeding your cat oily fish or a little butter to help lubricate the digestive system. If, after 24 hours, the cat's bowels have still not moved, take it to the vet who may administer an enema.

Facts About Neutering

Neutering is permanent sterilization; it involves the removal of the testicles in males and of the uterus and ovaries in females. It is now a very safe operation and causes little discomfort.

Benefits Neutering will benefit males and females far more that leaving them entire. It virtually eradicates the chances of prostate and testicular cancers and modifies behavioral problems such as spraying, roaming, and fighting. Females are unlikely to develop breast or uterine cancer, and unwanted gentlemen callers or the risk of pregnancy will no longer be a problem. Both males and females are less likely to stray, thereby reducing the risk of road and other accidents.

Veterinarians try to keep the cost of neutering down to a minimum to encourage people to have their pets neutered; if you still cannot afford this, there are organizations which offer very low-cost neutering.

Many thousands of unwanted cats are destroyed every year due to unplanned pregnancies. Reduce these numbers by having your cat neutered!

BELOW: Your cat will, in fact, benefit from neutering: behavioral problems such as spraying and aggression towards other cats will be considerably reduced.

First Aid

Cats are naturally inquisitive animals and often wander into danger, both inside the home and out of it. All owners of cats should be well prepared for potential emergencies and be ready to administer first aid which may be life-saving. When you first discover an injured animal, before touching it, make sure that you handle it in such a way as to avoid being bitten or scratched, as a frightened, injured cat is liable to behave out of character. Try to keep him as calm and as quiet as possible, when your first priorities will be to stop any bleeding and keep the animal breathing. Once stabilized, telephone the vet for advice, who will usually arrange for an immediate consultation. Wrap the injured animal in a blanket, keeping him secure, warm, and quiet and get him to the vet as quickly but as safely as possible.

Bites During fights, cats often scratch and bite one another. If your cat returns home and is showing signs of severe injury, you will need to take him to the vet. However, in most cases the injuries will not be too severe but merely minor wounds. Unfortunately, when a cat is bitten by another, harmful bacteria in the saliva gets into the wound. As soon as you become aware of a bite, bathe it regularly with salt water to keep the injury clean while it heals. This will minimize the likelihood of infection. However, it is more likely that you will not be aware of the injury. It is only after a few days, after the surface of the wound has healed up, that an abscess may develop underneath. This causes swelling and severe pain at the site of the wound. Usually the abscess will burst open, leaving a gaping hole which will need to be bathed regularly with salt water; you will need to consult your vet, who will usually prescribe antibiotics and may even stitch the wound. On discovering an abscess which has not burst, take the animal to the vet who will drain it and prescribe drugs.

Burns Cats usually steer clear of intense heat, but occasionally accidents do happen due to a spitting fire, or boiling water, or hot fat spilling over. Apply cold, running water to the affected parts for several minutes before seeking immediate veterinary attention. Do not apply anything else to the wound.

Chemical burns should be treated in the same way. Remember to protect your own hands with rubber gloves when handling the patient. If the chemical is known, it is important to report this information to your vet as this will have a bearing on his treatment of the injury.

Burns can also be caused by an electric shock, usually caused when a cat chews through an electric cable, when it is likely to suffer burns to the mouth. If you discover that your cat has been electrocuted, switch off the current before doing anything else. This will make the area safe for both you and your patient. If the cat is not breathing, he may require Cardio-Pulmonary Resuscitation, followed by veterinary attention.

Sunburn is a common hazard in sunny climes and prevalent everywhere in cats with white or light-colored ears. Make sure you use a sunblock especially formulated for cats with a very high sun protection factor. If you find that the ears are being repeatedly burned, you may have to keep him in when it is particularly sunny outside. If the condition seems severe, consult your vet immediately.

Choking There are any number of objects around the house and garden a cat can choke on, but chicken and fish bones are perhaps the most common. If he appears distressed, is pawing at his mouth, or even attempting to vomit, this should lead you to suspect that something is lodged in his throat. Before attempting to remove the object, you should first

RIGHT: Cats are by nature inquisitive creatures and despite their agility can occasionally get themselves into trouble. Accidents in the kitchen are usually burns-related, caused by hotplates and water boiling over. If your cat is accidentally burned, allow cold water to run over the affected parts and seek veterinary attention immediately.

restrain him by wrapping him firmly in a towel. Using a pair of tweezers, try to remove the object, but if you cannot, seek veterinary attention immediately.

Drowning It is rare for a cat to drown as they do not like water and will tend to avoid it. However, there is always an exception to every rule and cats occasionally fall into ponds and rivers. Once this happens, the lungs will quickly fill with water and the cat will stop breathing. After retrieval, and if the cat remains motionless, hold it upside-down by its back legs and swing it gently in front of you and back between your legs. Take care not to let the head touch the ground which could cause further injury. If the cat is still not breathing, use cardio-pulmonary resuscitation.

Road Traffic Accidents Every day, busy streets claim the lives of a large number of cats and injure even more, so if you live in a built-up area you should be mindful of all the dangers. If, in the harrowing

BELOW: Other than the Turkish Van, cats do not like water, so thankfully accidental drowning is rare.

ABOVE: From an early age cats love to climb, something which can occasionally get them into trouble.

situation that your cat is discovered at the roadside showing signs of injury, you should treat this as an emergency; it is important that you get the patient directly to a veterinary hospital without delay. External injuries are often immediately obvious and first aid to arrest bleeding is essential. Internal injuries may not be visible at all, but your vet will thoroughly check the cat over once he arrives in the hospital. Construct a makeshift stretcher from a coat and very carefully transfer the cat onto it, avoiding sudden movements. Keep him warm and quiet and the head slightly lower than the rest of the body to maximize the blood supply to the brain.

Sometimes, cats are involved in road accidents but still manage to get home. If your cat arrives home in a distressed state, there are some common indications which may suggest that this is what has happened, such as oil and dirt on his coat, broken or split claws, bleeding, hair loss, distressed breathing, pale gums, or broken limbs – these are just some of the signs. Keep the cat warm and still and rush him to the vet.

Falls Cats are great climbers and have an extremely good sense of balance, but it is their love of high vantage points which occasionally lands them in trouble. Fractures of the jaw and limbs are the most common injuries caused by falls, but less obvious internal injuries can also occur. If you see your cat fall and land awkwardly, or if you suspect injury due to a fall, seek veterinary attention at once.

Poisoning There are many different substances to be found around the house and garden which are poisonous to cats. However, cats are usually particular about what they eat and cases of poisoning are thankfully rare. The most common situation is when a cat eats a rodent which has itself eaten poison, when the effect on the cat will be most severe leading to coma and even death. Consult your vet immediately if you suspect this. Other substances, such as household medicines, can also be dangerous and it is important that you never administer to cats medicines or ointments prescribed for human beings. Garden chemicals are also a hazard and certain houseplants are also poisonous if eaten.

Shock Your cat could enter a state of shock for a variety of reasons, including poisoning, heatstroke, or as a result of an accident when he will appear weak and cold to the touch and his gums may be a pale grayish color. Keep him warm by wrapping him loosely in a blanket and call the vet at once.

Fractures If your cat is in severe pain and is loath to put weight on a leg, he may have broken it. It is most important to keep him as still and as quiet as possible as movement will cause more pain and damage. Lift him up gently, supporting the body but letting the damaged leg dangle. Consult the vet immediately. Do not attempt to make a splint for the injured limb – you could do even more damage. If you suspect a spinal injury, call the vet out to you.

Treating Wounds
Minor Wounds Clip the hair surrounding the wound, cleaning it thoroughly and treating it with an antiseptic. Consult the vet if you are at all anxious.

LEFT: Veterinary health care is expensive. It is always advisable to enroll in an insurance plan so that your cat's medical costs are covered should the need arise.

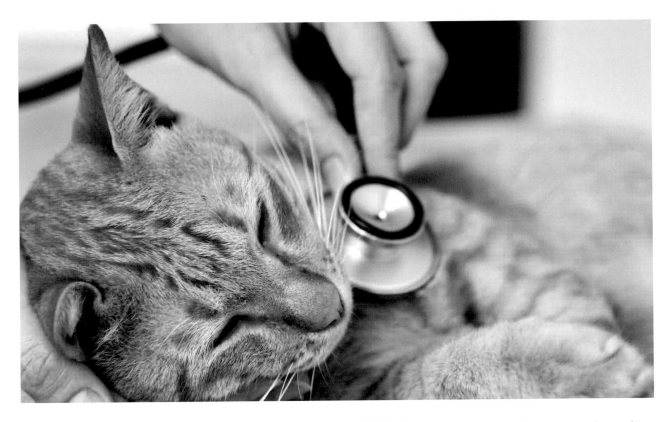

Deep Wounds If your cat has a serious cut which is exposing underlying tissue and bleeding profusely, and if the area can be bandaged, cover it with a thick pad of clean gauze, wrapping a bandage tightly around it to stem the blood flow. If the wound cannot be bandaged, hold the gauze over the wound and apply pressure. Do not apply a tourniquet, you could do even more damage. Rush the cat to the vet.

Arm yourself with a first aid kit for dressing minor wounds, etc.

Unconsciousness and loss of heartbeat

Check first to establish that the cat is alive. Place him on his side, clear his airway and bring his tongue forward. Establish if there are any broken bones and if so call the vet; if not, you may carefully pick him up and take him to the vet. If there are no signs of life (the cat is not breathing and has no heartbeat), administer cardio-pulmonary resuscitation (CPR).

Cardio-pulmonary resuscitation (CPR)

This is a combination of mouth-to-nose resuscitation and cardiac massage.

ABOVE: Modern veterinary medicine is very advanced today and treatments are very effective.

1. First remove any mucus or obstruction from the mouth or airway, pulling the tongue forward. Place your mouth over the cat's nose and breathe steadily into it for 2–3 seconds, waiting another 2–3 seconds for air to be expelled from the lungs.

2. If the cat fails to resume breathing and/or there is no heartbeat, you will need to apply cardiac massage. Place your hands on the chest just behind the elbow and press down firmly five times with a 1-second interval. Next, repeat the mouth-to-nose sequence, repeating it for 10 minutes or until the heart starts beating again.

3. Once the heart has restarted, cease cardiac massage but carry on with the mouth-to-nose resuscitation until the cat is breathing normally. This could take up to an hour. While you are proceeding with this, ask another person to call the vet for you.

Breeding

Breeding from your own cat is not something which should be entered into lightly. There are already many thousands of unwanted cats in rehoming centers, desperate for kind, loving homes, so producing even more is merely contributing to an already overwhelming problem.

Do not initiate the breeding process until you have firm homes for any kittens which may result, and

LEFT & ABOVE: Cats usually make excellent mothers and in the first few weeks will care for their kittens singlehandedly until they are old enough to commence solid foods.

remember that you, as a breeder, are morally responsible for keeping charge of them in the event of them being rejected by their new owners. Be aware also that it is far more difficult to rehome a non-pedigree than a pedigree cat, so breeding from a non-pedigree cat is definitely a labor of love and can never be for commercial gain.

Breeding pedigree cats is a different matter and breeders pride themselves on their cats' bloodlines, showing them off at cat shows and in magazines where the kittens are often advertised. Once again, don't expect to make a living from this; once stud fees, special dietary requirements for the mother and kittens, as well as registration fees, transfer fees, insurance, and vaccinations have been paid for, you will be lucky to break even.

Breeders who produce pedigree cats usually concentrate on a particular breed to which they are devoted, e.g. Siamese. However, reputable breeders would not encourage novices to breed from their own cats as they are only too aware of the pitfalls of passing on undesirable hereditary traits to future generations, and weakening the breed: you may find that when you buy a kitten it has already been placed on a non-active breeding register, meaning that you will not be able to register any of its offspring.

If you are determined to go ahead, and after carefully weighing up all the advantages and disadvantages, you will proceed to carefully plan the pregnancy.

Pregnancy and Kittening

Remember that you should never allow a female which is under a year old to become pregnant. It is assumed that you have done some research to find the perfect mate for your cat in the form of contacting the relevant society for your breed to discover reputable stud owners. Make sure that any potential mate is not related to your cat, as this is a sure way to pass on hereditary defects.

The stud owner will require your female to live in for at least a week and will ask you to supply vaccination and pedigree registration certificates; he will also check that your cat is registered for breeding. These are just some of the requirements before mating can take place.

Once the stud owner is satisfied that everything is in order, he will record all your relevant details and

BELOW & RIGHT: These charming tabby kittens are alert and aware of their surroundings – a sure sign of good health.

provisionally book your female in. This is the time to make known any of your cat's dietary preferences.

As soon as your female comes into heat and begins to call, phone the stud immediately and they will advise you when to bring her in. The stud owner will then keep a careful record of any matings which takes place and when be considers that it has been successful you may take your cat home.

The gestation period for a queen is 65 days; after three weeks her nipples will begin to swell, which is a sure sign that she is pregnant. At this stage, take her to the vet, who will recommend a special diet along with vitamin and mineral supplements. For the rest of her pregnancy you should give her the best possible care and once delivery seems imminent a nesting box in a quiet corner should be provided in which her kittens will be born. You may wish your vet to be present at the birth if you are at all anxious.

Care of the Kittens

It is more than likely that your cat will prove an excellent mother, taking sole charge of her kittens for the first few weeks, keeping them clean and feeding them herself. It is a good idea to keep the family in a confined area as the kittens will soon be on the move and eager to explore.

At around 5 weeks old, you should start to introduce them to solid food such as chicken and fish, offering tiny quantities at first, then at 6 weeks offer ready-prepared canned kitten food. At 9–12 weeks the kittens will be ready for their first vaccinations before going to the new homes you will have already found for them.

If this is the first and only time you are intending to breed from your cat, it is a good idea to have her neutered, when the risk of further pregnancies will be removed forever.

RIGHT: A beautiful Siberian with her young kitten.

All images in this book are in the public domain or have been supplied
under license by © Shutterstock.com.